EVERY CHOICE
is a
SEED

40 STORIES TO GROW YOUR LOVE FOR GOD

alicia britt chole

Every Choice is a Seed
40 Stories to Grow Your Love for God

© 2021 by Alicia Britt Chole

Published by onewholeworld, inc.
P.O. Box 323, Rogersville, MO 65742
www.aliciachole.com

Printed in the United States of America.

Library of Congress Cataloging-in-Publication Data

ISBN 978-0-9707454-2-2

Credits: Cover Photo by Jay Mantri @jaymantri. Cover design and interior layout by Kuhn Design Group. Back cover photo of Alicia Britt Chole by Sarah Carter Photography.

Heartfelt gratitude to Debra Boucher, Ruthie Jeter Gomez, Diane Marpe, Bethany Parrish, Rebekkah Richner, Stephanie Smith, and Whitney Crinklaw for their proofreading and encouragement.

Dedicated to my incredible mom.

You have been celebrating
all of my scribbles
since my first wobbly sentence.

You continue to be
the most generous soul
I have ever known.

Te quiero, Mamá.

La Hija.

CONTENTS

INTRODUCTION

"But I love this book!" my friend explained. "You've got to reprint it. My church needs it!"

The book under discussion was originally published in 2009 under the title *Intimate Conversations*. Written at the request of a family-focused ministry in search of a story-driven devotional, the little purple book went out-of-print (OOP) soon after the ink dried.

Staring at my publisher's letter that announced the book's OOP status, the abbreviation felt both poignant (piercing) and descriptive (just tack on an "s" at the end of OOP or a "p" at the beginning if you prefer). The news was disappointing. But thanks to God's mentoring, the news was not devastating.

A long time ago, He led me to write *devotionally*, i.e., *with* God and *for the love* of God. In other words, writing with Jesus grows my love for Jesus whether or not the words are read (let alone read widely) by others. Though *Intimate Conversations* would only be read by a few, writing the book—the months spent listening to God for the sermons in my ordinary life's stories—had surely grown me.

And then God, via the generosity of Koinonia Christian Church, commissioned a reprint. Such is the ever-surprising grace of God: it keeps giving, even beyond the grave.

For those of you who have read *Intimate Conversations* or my other books, I'd like to offer you a few notes to set the scene for *Every Choice is a Seed*.

- Unlike *Anonymous*, *The Sacred Slow*, and *40 Days of Decrease*, *Every Choice is a Seed* is story—not study—driven. The original request was for me to draw from my life as a child, parent, friend, and spouse to bring scriptural principles to life. True to the original commission, the tone of this reprint remains relational and conversational and inclusive of reflection and discussion questions to help the reader apply the principles to everyday life.

- When *Intimate Conversations* was published in 2009, my children were 12, 6, and 3, and my husband and I had been married 19 years. The last decade plus of living has filled my journal with stories. However, as a reprint, *Every Choice is a Seed* only contains stories from my early years of parenting, ministry, and marriage.

- Whereas *Intimate Conversations* was organized by conversation topics with God, *Every Choice* is organized as a series of chapters, each named for the specific choice under consideration.

Choices.

Every single one is like a seed planted in the soil of our present and, consequently, our future.

Life is filled to the rim with choice-seeds every waking moment, from the very second sleep releases us to greet a new day.

All of which means that we have more authority to shape our lives than we may feel we do.

Do you have the ability to choose which road to take to the store? Which coffee to order at the café? Which gift to buy for a friend? Then you have all the raw materials you need to choose which words you speak over loved ones, what thoughts you entertain in your mind, and what atmosphere you create in your soul.

And, you have two 24/7 mentors available to guide you: The Holy Spirit and the Word of God!

> "But the Advocate, the Holy Spirit, whom the Father will send in my name, will teach you all things and will remind you of everything I have said to you." (John 14:26)

> "The Word of God is alive and active. Sharper than any double-edged sword, it penetrates even to dividing soul and spirit, joints and marrow; it judges the thoughts and attitudes of the heart." (Hebrews 4:12)

> "If any of you lacks wisdom, he should ask God, who gives generously to all without finding fault, and it will be given to you." (James 1:5)

May this reprint be among the many tools God utilizes to reawaken His people to their God-given authority to choose well.

With you, for Him, in every choice,

Alicia

CHOOSE TO…

PLANT WELL

Choices.

We make them all day long.

> Through *deliberate decision*: "I have decided!"

> Through *passive postponement*: "I'll decide later."

> And through the *deception of denial*: "I don't need to decide because… it's not a problem, I'm okay, and I don't need help."

Each choice, however it is made, will do exactly the same thing: every choice will plant a seed.

And in the realm of choice—for better or for worse—every seed bears fruit.

What (on earth) are our choice-seeds growing? In our souls? In our health? In our families? At the office? Within our communities? Among the lost?

I often think of the power of seemingly small choices as I walk through our little plot of land in the Ozarks. Black walnut, white oak, silver maple, elm, birch, and an assortment of evergreens decorate our few acres in a wonderfully wild pattern. Each grew from some unassuming seed that settled into the soil a few years or decades ago.

Perhaps that is why we underestimate the power of our choice-seeds: individually they seem so unassuming and insignificant. One by one, they feel so small and unrelated. But from the tiniest acorn to the seed-packed pinecone, every seed (and every choice) has the ability to shape the landscape of our lives.

Whether through deliberation, passivity, or denial, our choices are shaping our legacies every moment of every day. May God help us take responsibility *for* all our choices so that the next generation will be blessed by what they inherit *from* all our choices.

Each of us brings a different backstory to our shared read of *Every Choice is a Seed*. Some of our pasts have been more immersed in crises. Some of our presents are more immersed in pain. Some of us have had choices stolen from us through abuse, accident, illness, injury, and loss.

But there is one choice that no one can steal from any of us: our choice to follow God.

So, let us set our hearts to follow Him with every choice we make!

Day after day,
     choice after choice,
          every choice is a seed,
               and in the realm of choice,
                    every seed bears fruit.

May God strengthen us to plant our choice-seeds well!

FOR REFLECTION AND DISCUSSION

"Choose for yourselves this day whom you will serve."
(Joshua 24:15)

One. Identify any choices you are currently making through *passive postponement* or *denial.*

Two. Picture your spiritual life like a plot of potential-filled land. What adjectives would you use to describe its current condition?

Rocky	Rich and ready
Flourishing	Recovering from pesticides
Carefully attended	Neglected
Weed-infested	Fruitful
Poorly guarded	Protected
Embarrassing	Joy-filled
Well-watered	Dusty and dry

Three. For change to be deep and lasting, our motivation must be God-centered. Consider the following prayer as together we recommit to taking responsibility for all of our choices and planting each choice-seed well.

Father God, You are trustworthy and merciful.
    You only reveal to heal.
Walk with me through my life,
    and grant me the courage to see what is growing there.
Transform me, not for perfection's sake,
    but so I can reflect You more accurately to a needy world.
Help me to plant my choice-seeds well as an offering
    of love to You.

LIVE EACH MOMENT WITH JESUS

Good morning, God, I'm so gra- (excuse me, God).

"You can have a snack after lunch."

I'm so grateful for th- (just a second, God).

"Your shoes are in the laundry room."

*I'm so grateful for this time we ha-
(sorry for the interruption, God).*

"They're there. Moooove things."

*I'm so grateful for the time we have together to-
(God, I think we'll have to continue this lat-).*

"Nooooo, please don't try to change baby's poopy diaper.

I'M COMING!"

Complete sentences. What a luxury.

This was one of the first things my friends commented on when I suddenly became a mother through the miracle of adoption at the age of thirty-one. My friends and I used to spend hours talking on the phone each week about the great mysteries of life. I was a highly focused conversationalist—a sincere listener who was rarely distracted.

But as a new mom? Well, I was still a sincere listener—I was continually listening for the sounds and (of greater concern) the non-sounds of my three children every waking (and sleeping) moment. Frankly, I think I missed half of what my friends said and it could take me minutes to complete a single sentence IF I did not forget what we were talking about in the first place.

In addition to giving me more empathy for those who live with attention-deficit disorders, that chronically-interrupted era of life provided an opportunity for me to reconsider how I nurtured relationships—with my husband, with my children, with my friends, and especially with my God.

Specifically, the new era revealed a weakness: I was too dependent on shared words, on well-formed sentences, and on neat and tidy blocks of time.

Parenting has confirmed an encouraging and ancient truth: intimacy with God is not on hold until I can complete grammatically-correct sentences in serene, aromatic spaces.

Each minute of every loud, distracting day is pregnant with potential for knowing God, if I can simply and intentionally live each minute *with* God.

Being with God was—and still is—the first priority of a disciple's job description:

> Jesus went up on a mountainside and called to him those he wanted, and they came to him. He appointed twelve—designating them apostles—that they might be

with him and that he might send them out to preach and
to have authority to drive out demons. (Mark 3:13–15)

The gospels record Jesus' conversations and teachings. However, a printed
page cannot fully depict what a 24/7 camera would have captured.

Most of Jesus' three years with the disciples were spent in daily prox-
imity, not in deep philosophical ponderings. Jesus and the Twelve
simply experienced life side-by-side. They walked together and worked
together, sat together and served together, preached together and were
persecuted together.

Doing life together was the disciples' key to knowing and becoming
like Jesus.

Right now, this same Jesus is *with* us. This same Jesus invites us to do
life *with* Him!

Every morning, God issues us a fresh, personal invitation to nearness.

(RSVP desired.)

FOR REFLECTION AND DISCUSSION

Yet, I am always with you.
(Psalm 73:23)

One. In this season of your life, how much can you relate to this devotional's starting prayer?

Two. What adjectives would you use to describe your prayer life?

Three. Jesus certainly set the example of private prayer times. But He
also set an example that is less quantifiable. He consciously lived each

moment connected to, and aware of, His Father. Spend a few minutes meditating on the following statements that Jesus made:

> "If anyone loves me, he will obey my teaching. My Father will love him, and we will come to him and make our home with him." (John 14:23)

> "Remain in me, and I will remain in you." (John 15:4)

> "As the Father has loved me, so have I loved you. Now remain in my love." (John 15:9)

Four. Consider the point made in the devotional about how Jesus and His disciples spent the majority of their time together. Make a conscious effort today to "see" Jesus with you, near you, in your daily life. Remember that He is with you while you are making your bed. Gratefully acknowledge His presence while you respond to an email. Smile at Him as you are stuck in traffic. God is with you.

(And He is happy about it!)

CHOOSE TO...

DO EVERY LITTLE THING FOR THE LOVE OF GOD

The *Practice of the Presence of God* is one of my most well-loved and well-worn books. From one of its discolored pages, Brother Lawrence's words still call to me:

> People seek for methods of learning to love God. They hope to arrive at it by I know not how many different practices…. . Is it not much shorter and more direct to do everything for the love of God, to make use of all of the labors in one's state of life to show Him that love, and to maintain His presence within us by this communion of our hearts with His? There is no finesse about it; one has only to do it generously and simply.[1]

Every-thing for the love of God.

Every-*thing* for the love of God.

Brother Lawrence goes on to say,

> In the way of God, thoughts count for little, love does everything. And it is not necessary to have great things to do. I turn my little omelet in the pan for the love of God; when it is finished, if I have nothing to do, I prostrate myself on the ground and adore my God, who gave me the grace to make it, after which I arise, more content than a king.[2]

Brother Lawrence was a monk in a monastery. I am a mother in Missouri. So what does "everything for the love of God" look like for me?

Through many changing seasons I have...

> mentored sincere souls for the love of God,
>
> changed countless diapers for the love of God,
>
> answered endless emails for the love of God,
>
> paid bills for the love of God,
>
> taught my children for the love of God,
>
> mourned the loss of dear ones for the love of God,
>
> hugged my husband for the love of God,
>
> cleaned my house for the love of God,
>
> watched stunning sunrises for the love of God,
>
> written devotionals for the love of God,
>
> taken naps for the love of God,
>
> forgiven others and myself for the love of God.

God accepted each act as worship! Love is what turns discipline into devotion. Love is what lights up the mundane with the miraculous.

So let us remember Him in every moment and "do every [little] thing for the love of God."

FOR REFLECTION AND DISCUSSION

And whatever you do, whether in word or deed,
do it all in the name of the Lord Jesus, giving
thanks to God the Father through him.
(COLOSSIANS 3:17)

One. Picture Brother Lawrence turning an omelet at the monastery for the love of God. Now picture yourself turning an omelet in your kitchen for the love of God. The monastery did not make the act into an offering of spiritual intimacy—Brother Lawrence's attitude did.

Two. Make a list of the small things you must do today. What would it be like to do them "for the love of God"?

Three. This principle opened up a world of new opportunities for me to develop intimacy with God. What changes might you experience as a result of integrating "every little thing for the love of God" more deeply into your life?

CHOOSE TO...

REST NEAR GOD

When our eldest transitioned to a "big" bed, we began a treasured tradition called "cuddle time." After the last bathroom stop, after the toothbrush was rinsed, after we prayed and sang "Jesus Loves Me," we simply cuddled and rested together.

Since Barry and I both worked from home, we were able to enjoy our kids' company all day long. But cuddle time at night was special, unique, and protected. The kids treasured the time together.

Lest anyone think that being quiet and still was ever natural for my kids, please understand that visitors always had a hard time believing we only had three children when the kids were younger because it sounded, and felt, like we had six.

As a quiet introvert, I have always been quite content in stillness and silence. But my tribe thrived with noise and movement.

Except during cuddle time.

Then Jonathan softly asked me penetrating questions. Keona dreamed with me about her future plans. Louie offered me his favorite car and looked deeply into my eyes.

And when talking ceased, little Jonathan would place his head near me to hear my heartbeat. Keona would sigh and ask me to rub her back. Louie would stay perfectly still not wanting the moment to end.

This was cuddle time. Its memory will forever be among the most precious jewels in my heart as a parent.

As the kids fell asleep, I would walk out the door with a sense that I had experienced something holy, something that reflected God's heart for me.

Surely His Father-heart treasures alone time with us! Surely He longs for us to curl up in a chair and rest with Him.

God is waiting for us to quiet our thoughts and listen for His heartbeat. He invites us to tell Him what we need and trust that He hears and is at work. He hopes that we will offer Him our physical treasures and look deeply into His eyes.

Though my kids are still wonderfully affectionate, our night-time ritual has transitioned to hugs, secret handshakes, and night-time prayers of blessing.

How grateful I am for us all that resting in God only gets sweeter and sweeter, and deeper and deeper, as the years go by.

FOR REFLECTION AND DISCUSSION

*He took a little child and had him stand among them. Taking
him in his arms, he said to them, "Whoever welcomes one of
these little children in my name welcomes me; and whoever
welcomes me does not welcome me but the one who sent me."*
(MARK 9:36–37)

One. Nothing can quite touch the experience of a child falling asleep in
your embrace. What adjectives would you use to describe how you feel
when a child sinks into your arms and drifts off to sleep?

Two. Take those adjectives and use them to describe how Father God
feels when you rest in Him: "When I become still and lean on God,
He feels _____."

Three. Tonight, before going to bed, try to carve out a few minutes to
become still enough, long enough, alone enough to sigh and whisper,
"Father, I love you."

CHOOSE TO...

BE PRESENT TO GOD

Fresh ink was on my daily planner. A glass of cool water sat upon my desk. My fingers were dancing across the keyboard when I felt—more than heard—God whisper to me: "Child, walk with Me. The day is new and My heart longs for you."

My fingers paused as I hesitated. Withdrawing from the swift current of that day's "to-do" list—as a spouse, parent, speaker, and mentor—was like resisting gravity.

Closing my eyes, I recalled the countless lost promises of "Soon, Father God, soon."

Then turning from the ocean of undone, I left the tasks on the desk and walked outside to be with my Creator.

The wet grass soaked the bottom of my pant legs as we walked together. The silence we shared was like breathing pure life. Then I sensed another question in my soul:

"Child, am I your Love or your business partner? You seem to find more value in being busy than in simply being."

"But, Father God," I countered, *"in the world, even in the church, busyness is a sign of commitment."*

"Yes, child. But commitment to whom? Commitment to what?"

The exchange caused me to question my pace: Why am I so busy? When did I begin to find value in a full schedule? What motivates my "yes" to tasks and to people?

My questions caused me to study: The voice of need always cried out to Jesus, yet He never seemed hurried, stressed, or driven. He disappointed many people to stay true to the purpose of His Father.

The study emboldened me to search my heart: *I am busy, but am I fruitful?*

And so a new chapter in my spiritual journey began. "Less busy, more fruitful" became my mantra. "Simplify and focus" became my means.

That conversation took place decades ago. Looking back, I now realize how that walk not only simplified my life, it *preserved* my life. Being wholly present, not hyper-productive, is the true key to spiritual health and fruitfulness.

FOR REFLECTION AND DISCUSSION

"Be still, and know that I am God."
(Psalm 46:10)

One. Which words, phrases, or concepts stand out to you from this chapter's reading?

Two. If someone unfamiliar with God were to describe—from observation alone without any explanations—your relationship with God, what words might they select? Would they see God as your Co-worker? Love? Coach? Critic? Friend? Santa Claus? Life? Source? Other?

Three. Does your schedule seem livable? If you could change three things about your schedule and pace, what would you select? Why?

Four. What would it cost—in time, money, and effort—to make these three changes?

Five. What will it cost—in your heart, health, family, and future—to not make these changes?

MAKE GOD MORE THAN FIRST

Early in my faith walk, a college Bible study on time management introduced me to the tool of *prioritization*. I found the concept both helpful and stressful.

Sitting in our small circle, a sheet of paper was placed before us and we were instructed to list the five most important things in our lives. Barely nineteen years old at the time, as I took up a pen to write, my interior conversation sounded something like this:

Number one? God! That was easy.

(I thought blissfully, beginning to write the next number on the page.)

Number two?

(Pause.)

Numero dos?

(Pause.)

Family? Service?

Others? Or work, which for me currently is school, right?

(Cue soft whirring in my brain, like a fan turning on to cool off an overheated computer.)

Church? The lost?

My heart? Or worship?

There's scriptural support for each of these. Maybe I'm overthinking this? I'll do it later as homework.

When everyone put down their pens, the leader handed us another "tool"—a weeklong time inventory. (Shudder if you can.) On this handy-dandy sheet, we were to log in EVERY ten minutes of our lives for two weeks. At the end, our instructions were to identify categories of how we spent our time, total up the amount of time spent in each category, and come ready to share anything we learned about ourselves.

Some in the group took the task less than seriously once informed that no one would ever see their tallies. It made no difference to me: I was on a mission. So for the next fourteen days, I painstakingly kept track of every minute and when finished with the totaling, I fell to the floor in tearful repentance.

> *Oh God! I still don't know what number two is, but it's obvious that number one is not You. If my first priority were You, I would spend more time with You than anything else. The results are clear: Forgive me! I serve the god of slumber!!*

True story.

Yes, I was a somewhat dramatic teen, suffering (no doubt) from too many carbs and too little sleep. But early on, I had a head-on collision with the limitations of prioritization.

In theory, prioritization enables us to evaluate opportunities and responsibilities in light of our values and primary needs. However, in practice, prioritization alone can lead us to focus on something, "complete" it, cross it off our list, and mentally go on with our day.

For example, in theory, a morning devotional may seem a worthy way to honor God as first in our lives. But that honor is only temporary if, in practice, we rise from our devotions, cross what is first (God) off our list as "completed," and go on to the next task without Him.

Long ago, God pressed me with a challenging question: "Alicia, who is the center of your life?" Without hesitation I answered, *"You are!"* His response stunned me, "No child, you are," He said. "You've made Me first, but you are still your own center."

I had *prioritized* God, but I had not *centralized* God. What a difference!

> When something is *centered*, it can never be completed or crossed off.
>   It can only expand.

> When something is *centered*, it cannot be confined by designations of "first," "second," or "third."
>   It is at the core of everything.

> When something is *centered*, it cannot be reduced to a task.
>   It becomes a living source and motivating force.

God wanted to be centralized in my life. Beyond first, He desired to be my center of gravity regardless of what I happened to be doing or what role I happened to be fulfilling.

He is my center of gravity as a daughter, spouse, and parent. He is my core as a speaker and writer. He is my motivation wherever I go and whenever I serve.

Is God first? Yes, but much more than first, He is at the center of all that I am and all that I do.

And that, for this over-thinking artist, was liberating indeed!

FOR REFLECTION AND DISCUSSION

"But seek first his kingdom and his righteousness, and
all these things will be given to you as well."
(MATTHEW 6:33)

Then I saw a Lamb, looking as if it had been
slain, standing in the center of the throne, encircled
by the four living creatures and the elders.
(REVELATION 5:6)

For the Lamb at the center of the throne will be their
shepherd; he will lead them to springs of living water.
(REVELATION 7:17)

One. Have you ever struggled to determine what should be first, second, third, fourth, and so on, in your life? If so, in what arenas of life does the ordering tension seem the most challenging?

Two. Write down your top five priorities. (I will spare you the time sheet—though it is an excellent exercise.) Instead of listing them numerically, attempt to draw them as five concentric circles. Start in the middle with the priority that most influences all others and work outward.

Three. These images in the above Scriptures from the book of Revelation are stunning! If Jesus is at the center in heaven, surely we want Him to be at the center of our lives here on earth. In your own words, what is the difference between prioritizing God and centralizing God?

Four. Over the next week, frequently remind yourself that in addition to being first, Jesus longs to be at the very center of your life. Note any changes you experience as you consciously acknowledge the centrality of God throughout your days.

CHOOSE TO…

TAKE TURNS
IN PRAYER

"Your son is autistic. He may never be able to speak or hold a conversation," said the neurologist. For years, we ached to hear Jonathan's words. At that time, we never imagined that one day, we would not only hear him speak, we would have the privilege of teaching him how to take turns speaking!

I attempted to illustrate the lesson at the ping pong table. Jonathan served me the ball and, instead of hitting it back, I caught it and held it. "Not taking turns is kind of like holding the ball," I explained. "It's hard to grow a friendship, when one person is always holding the ball."

True in conversation with humans, and true in prayer to God.

How free do you feel taking turns when talking with God? For many of us, turn-taking is much easier when we are full of faith than when we are full of questions. But taking turns is even more important when we have doubts, as the greats of our faith exemplify.

Abraham to God: "Will you sweep away the righteous with the wicked?" (Genesis 18:23)

David to God: "How long, O Lord? Will you forget me forever? How long will you hide your face from me?" (Psalm 13:1)

Jeremiah to God: "You are always righteous, O Lord, when I bring a case before you. Yet I would speak with you about your justice: Why does the way of the wicked prosper? Why do all the faithless live at ease?" (Jeremiah 12:1)

Abraham, David, Jeremiah.

Patriarchs, kings, and prophets all asked questions of God.

The difference between us and these forefathers is not that we have questions and they did not. The difference is that when they had questions, they took turns.

They asked… and then remembered God's Word.

They asked… and then listened for God's voice.

They asked… and then they waited.

Yet all too often,

We ask… and then remember our troubles.

We ask… and then listen to other voices.

We ask… and then we leave.

If we question without giving God a turn—if we question without waiting, listening, and remembering—we are in danger of cultivating resentment or arrogance.

But if we ask questions and then honor God by waiting, listening, and remembering, we cultivate dependence and humility.

And God's very Presence can answer our questioning hearts at depths words cannot penetrate.

FOR REFLECTION AND DISCUSSION

In the morning, O Lord, you hear my voice;
in the morning I lay my requests before you
and wait in expectation.
(PSALM 5:3)

One. On a scale of 1 (Never!) to 10 (I feel complete freedom), how easy is it for you to ask the kinds of questions Abraham, David, and Jeremiah directed to God?

Two. Personally, God most often speaks to me through the Bible, through the lives of my children, and through nature. When I am still, He inclines my thoughts in His direction and places principles and questions in my mind. How does God "speak" to you?

Three. Though few would describe God as "chatty," spiritually it is still beneficial to "take turns" when we speak with Him—to pause, to wait, and to listen. Today, as you conclude your devotional time, follow the example of David in Psalm 5:3. Lay your requests before God and then "wait in expectation."

CHOOSE TO...

LISTEN

Our eldest was born with a keen sense of sound. Noise startled him and any music with the exception of classical unsettled him. After being diagnosed on the autistic spectrum, we had Jonathan's hearing tested and learned that he heard sounds with a sensitivity that few humans shared. Today, Jonathan has perfect pitch and just completed a degree in Computer Animation, Music Composition, and Sound Editing!

Our middle was born with a keen zest for life. Noise soothed her and music inspired her. Endowed with extreme emotional intelligence and a deep love for others, Keona processed life out loud from the moment she was born. Today, she is a gifted listener and thinker who delights in physical expressions of love and service like dance and giving gifts.

The combination of their developing giftings made for many colorful days when they were young. One exchange in particular still stands out in my memory.

> "Keona," Jonathan moaned from upstairs, "please, can you just stop talking for FIVE minutes? I have a headache."

"Mommy says that talking is my gift," Keona retorted.

"It's a habit," Jonathan shot back.

"Gift!"

"Habit!"

"GIFT!"

"HABIT!"

(Then in stereo.) "M O M!!"

Our precious daughter loved to think out loud when she was little. Her words have always been meaningful and entertaining. She is a born communicator.

Soon after this exchange, language experts came to our home to evaluate our youngest for a speech delay. After spending several hours with us, the speech pathologist said, "There may be more going on, but my guess is that Louie doesn't talk because he doesn't need to talk."

"I'm not sure I understand," I replied.

Giving a less than subtle nod toward big sister, she said, "Louie isn't talking because perhaps other siblings are doing the talking for him."

"Ah," I said as I smiled at our gifted talker. Keona could read her brother like a book. Louie was more than happy to let his sister be his interpreter so that he could avoid explaining himself.

Extending grace to our daughter was easy. First, she was only five. Second, she was (and still is) absolutely delightful. Third, she reminded me of myself.

As an introvert, I have never been much of a talker in people's presence. But I do have a long history of being a talker in God's presence.

Early on, my "quiet times" were anything but quiet. My devotional life was a noisy, crowded one-way street of me talking to God.

Then discerning souls placed two books in my hands: Dick Eastman's *The Hour That Changed the World* and Richard Foster's *Celebration of Discipline*. (Whoever you are, I—and, no doubt, God—thank you profusely.)

These books introduced me to the discipline of silence and the art of prayerful waiting. And a whole new world opened before me!

Soon, that one-way street transitioned to a two-way street as I learned to listen while praying, to pause between questions, and to rest during worship.

Over the years I have discovered that—much like what margin on a printed page does for text—silence is what transforms words into communication.

FOR REFLECTION AND DISCUSSION

She [Martha] had a sister called Mary, who sat
at the Lord's feet listening to what he said.
(LUKE 10:39)

One. In *Creative Prayer*, Bridgid Herman stated the following:

> The most formidable enemy of the spiritual life and the last to be conquered is self-deception; and if there is a better cure for self-deception than silence it has yet to be discovered.[3]

Prayerfully think about the connection between noisy living and self-deception. How can silence unveil deception?

Two. Consider this passage from the Psalms:

> I wait for the Lord, my soul waits, and in his word I put my hope. My soul waits for the Lord more than watchmen wait for the morning, more than watchmen wait for the morning. (Psalm 130:5–6)

Earlier generations often spoke of waiting on the Lord. Is the waiting spoken of by the psalmist familiar or unfamiliar to you?

Three. Spend a few moments evaluating the "quiet" in your quiet time. Are you comfortable or uncomfortable with silence? What role does listening and silence have in your prayer life?

Four. Try an experiment. Carve out three to five minutes each day to simply be silent in God's presence. Focus upon an attribute of God and just *be*, without reading, speaking, asking, singing, or working. Honor God with a few minutes of stillness and then journal about your experience.

CHOOSE TO...

BE STILL

The doctors eyed my parents with suspicion.

"How did she cut her chin open *this* time?"

"In the bathtub," Mom and Dad replied sincerely. "She hates taking baths. She screams and squirms. We did our best to keep her safe, but she slipped out of our arms once again."

Strange but true.

I was a wiggler and a wailer in the bathtub as a toddler. My poor parents endured the neighbors' raised eyebrows, the doctor's questioning, and my pitiful puppy eyes as they held fast to their commitment to help me slough off the daily grime and emerge sparkling before bedtime.

Not that I had any special affinity for dirt.

Truth is, I loved being clean.

I simply did not like *the process*.

How much easier it would have been for all involved if I had just yielded and allowed my parents to get their cleansing hands on me. How much more quickly and painlessly we could have all arrived at their desired goal and my desired outcome if I had simply gotten *still*.

True then physically.

True now spiritually.

We all long to slough off the old and embrace the new: to become centered in God, at peace through His Word, and at rest in His love. But we struggle with letting God get His cleansing hands on us.

We are spiritual wiggle worms.

A few decades after my squirmy toddler days, ever-patient Jesus began to open my eyes to the strength of stillness.

He invited me to stop squirming, to resist wiggling, and to start relishing the ancient discipline of waiting on Him.

Peace is weatherproofed through stillness. Hope becomes muscular as we meditate on God's truth. Whether or not we tangibly sense His presence, our spirit is refreshed and renewed as we focus our thoughts on God.

The change we all long for is not found in going faster.

Lasting change is found in getting still.

FOR REFLECTION AND DISCUSSION

Be still before the Lord and wait patiently for him.
(PSALM 37:7)

One. This discipline of waiting is countercultural. After all, when was the last time you saw an advertisement using *It Goes Slower!* as a marketing hook?? When I was younger, a selling point for the quality of ketchup was how *slowly* it moved. The accompanying jingle sang a catchy, "an-ti-ci-pa-a-tion is making you wait." Now, even ketchup comes in speedy, squeezable bottles.

Our culture says that to get further you must go faster. But God's Word speaks of going slower to get deeper. How natural is it for you to *be still*? To *wait patiently*?

Two. Write down at least five qualities that you would like to describe your relationship with God in five years. How many of them will require time and/or patience to grow?

Three. "The change we all long for is not found in going faster. Lasting change is found in getting still." Summarize this principle in your own words and turn your summary into a prayer to God.

CHOOSE TO...

COME AWAY

"There's Jesus walking with Mommy," my son whispered to Barry while they watched from a distance as Sister Emmanuel and I walked up together along the gravel path. Wrapped in blue, her face radiated relationship with the living God. "Not Jesus, but Jesus' friend," my husband explained to our precious little boy.

Around five years old, Jonathan gazed up at Sister Emmanuel's beaming countenance and requested her hand. Together they escorted me to a tiny, tin cabin nestled in the trees. Confident that mommy was safe, Daddy and son gave me kisses and left me in the cabin-turned-chapel for two days of prayer.

Unpacking in silence, I recalled my first prayer retreat. Years ago, I considered these times of focused prayer a luxury. Now my husband and I are convinced that prayer retreats are a true necessity for our family.

A wobbly desk, a fraying patch of carpet, bare walls—the simplicity of the place stood in stark contrast against the neon and clutter of our world.

Slowly, hour by hour, the solitude increased my awareness that I am never alone.

Reading.

Listening.

The God who is always near soothed my anxious heart with His Word. His truth was like warm oil on my dry spirit.

Writing.

Walking.

Relaxing in God's presence.

Resting in God's acceptance.

Simultaneously I knew my sinfulness and God's love. Such gracious love warrants gratitude-filled pauses in our days and life.

Waiting.

Waiting on God.

Waiting because God is worthy of our waiting—whether or not He speaks.

The treasures of waiting are many, but the greatest of these is God Himself.

My hope is that through these sacred spaces of prayer-filled pauses, more of Jesus will be visible through me. My hope is that, even without a godly saint by my side, my children at every age will be able to say, "There's Jesus. He walks with my mommy."

FOR REFLECTION AND DISCUSSION

"Come with me by yourselves to a quiet place and get some rest."
(MARK 6:31)

One. Henri Nouwen suggested that we dedicate "an hour a day, an afternoon a week, a day a month, and a week a year"[4] to prayer retreats with Jesus. "What a dream!" we sigh. But all dreams begin with a breath. All walks begin with a step. Take a few moments to ask Jesus how you could carve out more alone time in your life. Write down your thoughts and begin to make plans toward your retreats whether they be for fifteen minutes or several days.

Two. What attitudes currently reflect your approach to, and time with, God? Duty or discovery? Habit or hope? God is infinitely creative. He is speaking, He is waiting, and He is longing for us to discover Him anew every day.

Three. Conclude your discovery time with God in silence. Unlike other forms of meditation, Christian meditation is not an emptying of our minds but a focusing of our thoughts exclusively on God. Begin thinking of adjectives that describe God (pure, trustworthy, near, etc.) and then wait before Him, letting those adjectives simmer in your soul. As sleep refreshes our bodies, silence refreshes our spirits.

VALUE THE LESS VISIBLE

"Alicia, I know that I am doing the most important thing on earth in caring for my baby. I feel awful even saying this. But why do I feel so, so—" She paused, searching for words. Finding one, she offered it with a wince, "unproductive?"

Bright, gifted, and extremely capable, this dear woman was using her framed master's degree as a paperweight. She was stewarding the miracle in her arms with devotion and feeling like the world was passing her by.

Whether or not we have diaper rash cream in every room of the house, most of us have experienced (or will experience) chapters of life that did not utilize our professional skills and training.

We have postponed schooling, hopped off the career ladder, declined advancement, and chosen a less-driven pace to focus on something we deem "better."

When obedience leads us into such seasons, what does productivity look like? When our résumés are not growing, what is?

In a word: *character*.

Of course, visible seasons are also filled with the opportunity to develop character. But when obedience to God leads us to decrease visibly in what the world sees and applauds, that decrease creates a unique opportunity to increase spiritually in what God sees and applauds.

The challenge is, however, that productivity looks different in such seasons.

> Instead of being praised for completed projects, we are given countless opportunities to make peace with the incomplete.

> Instead of being promoted for being first, we are given numerous opportunities to find joy in being last.

This different type of growth reminds me of the counsel I received from an opportunity to meet with a fitness trainer long ago. He explained that at first, when I was beginning my new fitness routine, it would feel like I was really making progress, because the initial fat burn would be easily visible.

"Then," he cautioned, "you'll come to me and ask what's wrong because you're not seeing as much change. Don't be fooled and don't be discouraged. That's when the real work is occurring. It means you're starting to build muscle."

Building muscle, like building character, is a different type of productivity.

> It is less visible.

> And more powerful.

> In fact, character growth is the real work of life.

FOR REFLECTION AND DISCUSSION

*We also rejoice in our sufferings, because we know that suffering
produces perseverance; perseverance, character; and character, hope.*
(ROMANS 5:3–4)

One. In your own words, summarize this parent's struggle regarding productivity. Is this challenge in any way familiar to you? In what way?

Two. In the above passage in Romans, the Greek word translated as sufferings (*thlipsis*) is more often translated as trouble(s). Looking back over the last year, are you able to identify some "troubles" that produced character in you?

Three. Consider again the wisdom in the fitness trainer's words. Then conclude by thanking God for how He is building muscle (character) in you currently through your circumstances. This invisible work of character growth is a form of productivity that will outlast this lifetime.

CHOOSE TO…

SEE THE
SACRED SMALL

"But Mom, it's for the church!" pleaded my sleep-deprived son. "Doesn't that make it holy??"

Jonathan had gone way (W A Y) beyond anything any of us had imagined to create a customized video game for the youth game room. His innate, artistic perfectionism had hijacked his sincere longing to make a contribution and kept him up for days in an attempt to meet a self-imposed deadline.

He was utterly exhausted but did not want to give up on his commitment, so he tried to persuade me to approve another all-nighter…in the name of all that was "holy."

What activities in life are *holy*?

What makes a deed an act of *worship*?

The Oxford English Dictionary defines *holy* as, "Kept or regarded as inviolate from ordinary use, and appropriated or set apart for religious use or observance; consecrated, dedicated, sacred."[5] The word comes to us through the Old High German *hail* which speaks of health, wholeness, and well-being.

Merriam-Webster defines worship as, "to honor or show reverence for as a divine being or supernatural power."[6] The word comes to us from the Middle English *worpschipen* which speaks of respect for a deity.

> Is being a pastor automatically more holy than being a parent?

> Is singing necessarily more worshipful than cleaning?

> Is serving always more honorable than sleeping?

I do not think so.

> Our motivations can make the simplest task holy or the most impressive deed dead.

> Our attitudes can make the smallest act worship or the grandest offering bankrupt.

This is cause for celebration among the sincere in heart. Every season of life and every single daily deed is overflowing with potential to live a holy, worshipful existence.

> When I was single, solitude was *holy*.

> When God's path led me into marriage, two-now-one was *worship*.

> When I became a mother, life together was *sacred*.

This lesson was embedded deeply in my soul as a new parent.

As the sun rose each day, all three children would climb into bed with us one-by-one. Keona normally came in first, carrying her pillow and wedging herself between Barry and me. She snuggled close, and I would take in the refreshing scent of her peppermint hair cream.

Then Jonathan would emerge sleepily from his room and say, "Morning!" Crawling onto our bed, he would close his eyes as I kissed his warm, porcelain face and remembered how he used to fit in my hands.

The next ten to thirty minutes would be filled with quiet family cuddles and curious questions about life until wiggly baby Louie woke up. Then we would bring him to our bed and all become happy fences around him to keep him safe.

This was quite a departure from our first seven years of marriage. In those earlier years, Barry and I would always get up and offer the first part of the day to God through songs, walks, extended readings, and quiet times. Without question, parenthood altered that pattern significantly.

But I remember talking with God while gazing into the eyes of my loving kids, touching their soft faces, and looking at the clock. My Bible, journal, and piano would still be waiting for me later in the day. And I knew that Father God was smiling over these morning moments.

I could almost hear His whisper as I hugged and loved on His kids: "Ah, this too is holy. This too is worship."

Lost in thought, my pause of remembrance was a bit too long for Jonathan, so he repeated his question, "Mom, it's for the church. Doesn't that make it holy?"

And I said, "My love, exhaustion isn't a sign of devotion. What makes things holy is why we do them. Always remember: your life is a gift from God. Taking care of that life is a form of worship. Sleep is holy too."

FOR REFLECTION AND DISCUSSION

And whatever you do, whether in word or deed,
do it all in the name of the Lord Jesus, giving
thanks to God the Father through him.
(Colossians 3:17)

"Truly I tell you, whatever you did for one of the least of
these brothers and sisters of mine, you did for me."
(Matthew 25:40)

One. "Whatever you do…" Look back over the past twenty-four hours and remember the small things you did in honor of God.

Two. Whether or not others noticed, God saw and received everything you did "for the least of these" as an offering of love. However, when we feel that His "well done" is not enough, we can slip into martyrdom, serve resentfully, and perhaps even begin to emotionally punish others for not noticing our sacrifices. Take a few moments in prayer to give God the opportunity to address any sourness sabotaging your service.

Three. Now, consider what awaits you in the next twenty-four hours. Ask God to open your eyes to the sacred small, to the holy hidden in your every-day life.

CHOOSE TO...

SAVOR IN-BETWEEN SPACES

This is reality, not humility: I was a pitiful surfer.

And, apart from hurricane season, South Padre Island in Texas was not necessarily known for its surf, which made my lack of skill even more lacking.

Nonetheless, every weekend—weather permitting—I would strap my six-foot-two-inch, twin fin, Danny (or was it Tony?) Holt New Image surfboard onto the truck and drive an hour to the beach.

Pulling up to the shore, I would drink in the sea breeze, wax up my board, head into the water… and most of the time it would end there with me sitting or floating on the board as a wannabe surfer girl.

However, from time to time I would actually try to catch a wave and— if feeling especially adventurous—even attempt going beyond one set of waves to catch a bigger set on the other side.

That pilgrimage from smaller to larger waves required a great deal of upper body strength. I had to stay balanced on the board and use my arms as paddles to slice through the first break and reach the calm before the next set of waves hit.

The pros (well, most people) did it effortlessly. But not me. I swallowed gallons of saltwater, found myself under the board as much as on top of it, and had a knack for navigating straight into—as opposed to through—crashing sets of waves.

However, once in a while I would emerge exhausted on *the other side.*

This oasis between breaks offered a few moments of rest. Another set of waves was coming for sure. Undoubtedly, they would be bigger, stronger, and require more skill to ride.

But for a minute
    there was a calm
        to take a deep breath,
            recover from what was,
                and prepare for what was to come.

That image has often mentored me throughout the years, and especially now, many years removed from my high school days at South Padre Island.

Now (when teenagers call me "ma'am" and with a gasp shout, "*You* were a surfer???") the memory of my surfer days returns as I find myself in between breaks in the ocean of real life.

The last set of waves was a challenge to navigate—extremely fruitful, and extremely full. Here, I find myself in between what was and what will be, in the pause before a transition in life and ministry.

And in this pause, I sense Father God whispering, "Rest, my child. Do not strain to see the next set of waves. Do not stress over whether you will be able to ride them well. Do not wonder if they will be more this or less that. Simply rest."

Logically, the next set of waves you and I will face in our lives will be stronger, bigger, and require more skill to navigate. Here, however, guessing what will be is not our primary concern. The calling of those who are "in between" is to wait faithfully and rest intentionally.

Divine pauses are rich with potential. Whether they last a few weeks or a few years, these lulls are gifts from God.

FOR REFLECTION AND DISCUSSION

*Teach us to number our days aright,
that we may gain a heart of wisdom.*
(PSALM 90:12)

One. Where would you place yourself in this illustration?

- Trying to navigate a new set of waves.

- In the lull between the last set and the next set of waves.

- Staring at the next set of waves, wondering if you should turn around and head back to the car.

- Under the board, swallowing sand.

- Out to lunch.

Two. Sometimes lulls can last so long that they feel like oceans in and of themselves. In such seasons, it is tempting to expend energy wondering what lies ahead. Think back on your most recent challenging season. Did you enter it rested? In what specific ways do you think being rested might benefit your next challenging season?

Three. If you currently find yourself "in between," consider adding something from the following list to your plans for rest and renewal.

Take time to pamper your soul.

> Go on a prayer retreat.
> Begin a new devotional book or Bible study.
> Start a gratitude journal.
> Listen to worship music.

Soberly evaluate and enhance your state of health.

> Take a class on healthy eating.
> Consult a trainer.
> Begin an exercise plan.
> Get a therapeutic massage.

Nurture friendships.

> Reconnect with a dear old friend.
> Ask someone new to join you for coffee.
> Write a thank-you letter to a teacher or mentor.
> Establish a daily walk and talk with Jesus.

Expand your mind.

> Enjoy an art class.
> Sign up for music lessons.
> Visit your library.
> Listen to a new podcast.

Attend to loose ends at a peaceful pace.

> Organize photos.
> Purge a closet.
> Finish a project.
> Mend something broken.

Or _____?

CHOOSE TO...

TRUST THE FATHER

"Why?!!" the kids cried as Barry relayed the sad news that their overnight plans with the grandparents had to be cancelled.

Extreme disappointment is often immune to logic. Barry knew that this was not the moment to launch into a scientific explanation of why freezing rain makes road conditions dangerous. The kids' mounting unrest would not be dissolved by charts and graphs.

"WHY?" they asked again with increased volume and tears in their voices.

Extreme disappointment is predictably lacking in patience. Barry knew this was not the moment to put the teakettle on the stove and invite the kids to evaluate their emotions while meditating on Claude Debussy's "Clair de Lune." The kids' mounting unrest would not be defused by discussion, culture, and a hot cup of tea.

So Barry paused, looked lovingly into their eyes, and simply said, "Let me show you why. Everyone put your shoes on."

This was unexpected.

Action? Something physical?

Their disappointment temporarily distracted by a task, the kids quickly put their shoes on, as Dad opened the door.

Having an innate aversion to cold temperatures (as in, say, under 75º F), I went to watch from the upstairs window. Whines of frustration quickly gave way to squeals of delight as the kids slipped and slid over the driveway.

Barry gave them a few minutes to play and then said, "This is why. If you can't walk on the road, it's not wise to drive on the road."

They were convinced.

He allowed them to feel the logic, instead of just hear the logic.

He had the patience to reveal the answer when they did not have the patience to hear the answer.

And he was not done yet.

Surprising even me, Barry then leaned over the car's window and in the growing ice carved out a tic-tac-toe grid.

They took turns for one short game and, without even so much as a whisper, Daddy was saying, "And we can still have fun."

I never heard another whimper about the change of plans.

Wise dad? Absolutely. And also a principle to remember next time we are disappointed.

Often we wonder why God does not simply explain things to us. "Surely our disappointment would dissolve if He would just tell us the why behind His actions and choices," we moan.

Instead, God often seems silent in our moments of greatest frustration. Even then, God is near. He is wisely withholding His words knowing that extreme disappointment is rarely tamed by logic or lecture.

If we listen, we may hear Him inviting us to put on our shoes and go outside—to do something physical and seemingly unrelated.

If we watch, we may find Him holding our hand, while we slip about and see something unexpected.

Reminding ourselves of God's faithful, fatherly presence can take the edge off (and the sting out of) our disappointment long before anything logical can fill in the empty blanks of our angst.

Truly, God is the wisest Father of all.

FOR REFLECTION AND DISCUSSION

Good and upright is the Lord;
therefore he instructs sinners in his ways.
He guides the humble in what is right
and teaches them his way.
All the ways of the Lord are loving and faithful
for those who keep the demands of his covenant.
(PSALM 25:8–10)

One. How do you respond—emotionally, physically, or spiritually—when you are deeply disappointed? Do you, for example, pout? Sleep? Fear that the world is coming to an end? Get grumpy? Withdraw?

Two. Drawing from your experience with children, what is the wisest response when someone is irrationally frustrated? Has God ever used this response with you?

Three. Sometimes disappointment's power is in its vagueness. Write down as specifically as you can anything you are currently disappointed about.

Four. Then bring each disappointment before God in prayer. Affirm in faith that He is indeed a wise Father. Ask Him to help you grow in recognizing His fatherly presence even in the midst of frustration.

FIND HOPE
IN GOD'S GRIP

Unplanned. Unwanted. One day, the unexpected occurred.

Ever since she could remember, little Teresa loved holding her daddy's finger as they walked together. She held on tightly determined to never let him go. She knew if she stayed by his side, all would be well.

Then one day, as they were walking to their waiting car, Teresa looked up to see a truck racing through the parking lot.

There was no time: the truck was moving too fast.

There was no escape: she would be hit.

Without even thinking, she did what she thought she never would do.

In fear, little Teresa let go of her daddy's finger.

But little Teresa's daddy was a good father. He expected the unplanned.

He anticipated the unwanted. He had seen the truck before little Teresa had felt the first tremor of fear.

And all along, while Teresa held on to her daddy's finger, her daddy had wrapped his hand firmly around her wrist.

> As the truck sped toward Teresa, her daddy tightened his grip.

> As Teresa let go in fear, her father lifted her up and carried her to safety.

> Then her daddy held Teresa in his arms while fear loosened its hold on her heart.

> (As I said, he was a good daddy.)

We too hold tightly to our Father God's finger, determined to never let Him go, confident that our commitment, our experience, and our intellect are the forces that alone bind us to our God.

Then the unexpected occurs. Unplanned, unwanted, in fear we feel our hold loosening as pain presses us and the unknown casts shadows on our soul.

But all along, our faithful Father has firmly gripped us by His Spirit. He is the author and guardian of our faith.

In the time of trouble, He tightens His invisible yet eternal grip on us and carries us to safety. Then Father God offers to hold us in His arms while fear loosens its hold on our hearts.

Safe in His arms, we gratefully, with reaffirmed childlike faith, echo the confidence of David the psalmist:

You hem me in—behind and before; you have laid your hand upon me. Such knowledge is too wonderful for me, too lofty for me to attain.... If I rise on the wings of the dawn, if I settle on the far side of the sea, even there your hand will guide me, your right hand will hold me fast. (Psalm 139:5–6, 9–10)

FOR REFLECTION AND DISCUSSION

You hem me in—behind and before.
(PSALM 139:5)

One. Wrapped securely around your intellectual, emotional, and experiential hold on faith are the presence and power of God Himself. Perhaps recent events have unnerved you and loosened your grip on faith. Meditate on the truth that, like the father in this devotional, God saw what was coming and activated His power to keep you long before you felt the first tremor of fear.

Two. The parking lot story is an adaptation of an experience relayed to me by one of my first pastors. Like Teresa, we need to treasure the One who holds our hand. Picture God's strong hand gripping your wrist as you hold tightly to His finger.

Three. Conclude your time of reflection by reading the passage below and recommitting your unknown future to God's care:

Let us fix our eyes on Jesus, the author and perfecter of our faith, who for the joy set before him endured the cross, scorning its shame, and sat down at the right hand of the throne of God. Consider him who endured such opposition from sinful men, so that you will not grow weary and lose heart. (Hebrews 12:2–3)

VIEW YOUR PAIN THROUGH HIS CROSS

"I wouldn't have written the script of my life this way, my God."

"What would you have changed, Child?"

"I would have deleted unnecessary pain."

"What kind of pain is that?"

"Senseless misunderstandings, incurable illnesses, and undeserved injustice. These produce nothing but tears in my heart and aches in my soul. I could have done without them."

"I too could have done without sin's shadows and pain's piercings. But because of choices made long ago and choices remade every moment, I myself had a choice to make: turn my back on sin's shadows or personally embrace pain's piercings."

"What did You choose, my God?"

"I chose the path of what you call 'unnecessary' pain."

"Why?! How?"

"Actually, you helped Me. Before you were born, Child, I saw you and My love for you was greater than life. Through sweat and blood I measured My love for you and its strength fixed My life willingly to a cross. By embracing pain, I robbed sin of its power to crush you."

"Then the shadows will not destroy me! But there are still aches in my heart and tears in my soul."

"Yes, Child. In Mine as well. But even there you can find treasure if you allow the tears in your heart and the aches in your soul to grow dependence on Me in your spirit."

FOR REFLECTION AND DISCUSSION

And we know that in all things God works for the good of those who love him, who have been called according to his purpose.
(ROMANS 8:28)

One. This tender dialogue between Creator and Child reflects on soul-bruises. If we think of our lives as a movie, all of us have scenes we wish could have been deleted or edited. These are the bruising memories that cause us to wince, to ache, to question, and to move faster.

When you remember these scenes (intentionally or unintentionally), where is God in the picture? Absent? Present? Do you picture Him watching? Sleeping? Helping? Protecting? Distracted? Critiquing?

Take a few moments to consider the truth that God was and is as near to you as a mother is to the child in her womb.

Two. In this story, God speaks of how His love for His child fastened His life to the cross. Consider the truth that God's intense love for you strengthened Him to endure pain so that you could know freedom: "For God so loved the world that he gave his one and only Son, that whoever believes in him shall not perish but have eternal life." (John 3:16)

Three. This devotional suggests that dependence is a holy outcome of pain. In a culture that applauds independence, valuing dependence can be a challenge. Choosing to be dependent on God is a vote—not for passivity or weakness—but for active reliance. Through dependence, we intentionally immerse ourselves in God's strength.

In the coming days, remind yourself that fruit can be cultivated even in the place of pain when we view our trials through His sacrifice.

REMEMBER YOUR REDEEMER

When Keona was barely four, she found a spider on the bathroom floor. Spiders have never been among her favorite of God's creatures. But we have brown recluses in Missouri and this spider carried the tell-tale violin shape.

So, after squishing the spider soundly, I proceeded to pick up the pair of pants I had laid out for Keona and run my arms through the legs.

"Mommy, what are you doing?" Keona asked.

"I'm running my arms through the pant legs so that if there are any other spiders, they'll bite me instead of biting you," I explained.

Her response took me by surprise.

With moist eyes, Keona said, "You'll take the spider bite for me?"

"Of course," I whispered, realizing that this was a love-in-action picture for my daughter.

Keona thought for a few seconds, winced, and turned to me again with tears rolling down her cheeks.

"Mommy," she asked, "What if I'm not strong enough to take the spider bite for my children? Will you take it for them too?"

Wrapping my arms around her, I said, "Yes, my love. As long as I have breath, I will do everything I can to take the spider bites."

It felt like a holy moment with my girl and for me; one of those impossible to plan lessons etched in both our hearts. And it was a lesson not soon forgotten.

Many years later, Keona was telling me about a dream she had in which she was attacked by a mean tiger. "That sounds scary," I empathized. "What happened next?" "Oh, it was okay," she replied calmly. "You took the tiger bite."

Yes indeed, while I have breath.

Just as my Jesus did for me.

On the cross, Jesus took upon Himself the stench of sin and sting of death. He took the spider bites for us all so that we could live free and fearless with God.

Perhaps you did or you did not have a parent who could offer to take the spider bites of life for you. But you do have a Savior who took upon Himself the sins of the world before you even took your first breath.

Do not be afraid, my friend.

Remember your Redeemer.

Greater is He who is in you than He who is in the world. (1 John 4:4)

FOR REFLECTION AND DISCUSSION

*"Greater love has no one than this, that he
lay down his life for his friends."*
(JOHN 15:13)

One. Whom would you "take the spider bite" for? Pray for each one as you list them by name.

Two. Who would "take the spider bite" for you? Thank God for each one as you list them by name.

Three. Jesus, ultimately, took sin's bite for us. Consider the following words and allow thanksgiving to well up in your heart for Christ's love and sacrifice:

> When they hurled their insults at him, he did not retaliate; when he suffered, he made no threats. Instead, he entrusted himself to him who judges justly. He himself bore our sins in his body on the tree, so that we might die to sins and live for righteousness; by his wounds you have been healed. (1 Peter 2:23–24)

ASK FOR LIVING WATER

Years ago, our area went through a difficult dry season.

With eyes fixed heavenward, I kept watching storm clouds race across the sky like silent stampedes of silver gray stallions. Day after day after day, they carried the hope of rain… away.

Along with other concerned watchers, I sighed and offered silent prayers for relief. We all longed for life-giving water.

Extended droughts create visible crises in our land. But another form of drought actually leaves us far more vulnerable to disaster.

Have you felt the pain of drought in your soul?

> When hope has been carried away to another place.
>
> When emotions are brittle and snap under pressure.
>
> When sleep is diminished by a gnawing fear.

When no place and no thing can quench a thirst
deep within.

The Samaritan woman described in John 4 was well-acquainted with
drought of the soul. Broken relationships, secrets, rejection, whispers—
her last reserves of hope were depleted by disappointment years ago.
Standing in the sun by a weathered well, her hands were wet but her
heart was dry.

Suddenly, Jesus spoke to her, "Will you give me a drink?"
(John 4:7)

Startled, she bowed her head, glancing down to avoid His eyes. His
words trespassed propriety twice: Jews (His people) did not associate
with Samaritans (her people), and most respectable people did not
associate with someone "like her" at all.

Yet He had asked, so she dared to speak, "You are a Jew
and I am a Samaritan woman. How can you ask me for
a drink?" (John 4:9)

The stranger answered, "If you knew the gift of God
and who it is that asks you for a drink, you would have
asked him and he would have given you living water."
(John 4:10)

A gift? From God? Of living water? Nonsense, she thought, as her hands
tightened around the worn rope to pull up a bucket from the well.

Motioning with His hand toward the well, the stranger
continued, "Everyone who drinks this water will
be thirsty again, but whoever drinks the water I give
him will never thirst. Indeed, the water I give him will
become in him a spring of water welling up to eternal
life." (John 4:13–14)

Lifting her head, surely she studied the stranger. His garments, like hers, were simple. Rough sandals covered calloused feet. Perhaps there was nothing noteworthy about Him, except for His eyes. As He spoke of water, my guess is that His eyes shone like the sea—warm, deep, and full of ancient wisdom.

> "Sir," she asked, "give me this water so that I won't get thirsty and have to keep coming here to draw water." (John 4:15)

Their conversation navigated uncomfortably through her past failures, present traditions, and future hopes. Listening, she began to wonder, *Who is this stranger? Surely this is no ordinary man. Probably a teacher, perhaps a prophet, or—or—could he be the Messiah?!*

> Then Jesus declared, "I who speak to you am he." (John 4:26)

With these words, the bucket slipped from her fingers. She stood speechless, staring into Jesus' eyes. Then, deep within, her spirit knew what her mind could not yet comprehend: Living Water stood before her!

Is your soul thirsty? Does your heart feel parched deep within?

Jesus' offer of living water still stands. With tears, He has traced every brittle crack in our dry hearts. In the scorching heat of shame, in the blistering desert of regret, God Himself offers to cover us like a welcome cloud. He longs to release within us His sweet, strong, living rain of truth.

Will that release transform the scenery, the circumstances, of our lives?

> *Unknown.*

Will that release transform our very souls?

> *Guaranteed.*

Drought in our land is out of our hands. But drought in our hearts must begin its retreat at the sound of three simple words, "Jesus, I believe."

FOR REFLECTION AND DISCUSSION

Jesus answered, "Everyone who drinks this water will be thirsty again, but whoever drinks the water I give him will never thirst. Indeed, the water I give him will become in him a spring of water welling up to eternal life."
(JOHN 4:13–14)

One. Drought can be devastating. Take a moment to remember a time in which you experienced drought physically or spiritually.

Two. Replay Jesus' interaction with the Samaritan woman in your mind. What emotions might she have felt at the moment she realized who Jesus really was? How do you think her realization and reaction made Jesus feel?

Three. A few chapters later Jesus said, "If anyone is thirsty, let him come to me and drink. Whoever believes in me, as the Scripture has said, streams of living water will flow from within him." (John 7:37–38)

Are you thirsty today? If so, turn to Jesus in prayer. His offer of living water has yet to expire.

CHOOSE TO...

LISTEN TO YOUR BODY

The dishes were the last straw for me.

My husband and I had been burning the candle at both ends for over a decade. As single ministers (he in Texas and I in the Far East), we stayed up late, ate irregularly, exercised infrequently, always said yes, and never thought about it because we were so very thrilled to simply partner with Jesus in the Great Commission. When we married, we continued this pace as we poured out our lives for the love of university students.

Then a transition occurred where we needed to spend one year in constant travel to gather a team of committed individuals and churches who would partner with us for the next season of ministry.

Many churches may be familiar with this model of missionary itineration. The rationale behind the practice is that it keeps the faces and work of the missionaries fresh in the minds of those who support them, and it provides the opportunity for young and old to hear a call to serve.

In theory, it is truly beautiful.

In practice, it is insane unless you happen to be graced with hyperactivity and outrageous extroversion.

I am not.

As the miles clicked on the odometer, something else was clicking within me—a countdown to burnout.

Within six months, I felt like a zombie.

Living out of a suitcase, having personal conversations with people who were absolute strangers less than an hour before, searching for hotels at midnight, and eating way too many meals at inexpensive diners did not make for healthy living physically or emotionally for my wiring.

Genetically far sturdier, Barry was tired but not at the point of collapse. He drove us from place to place while I tried to nap or read or listen to worship. One day when we were home, Barry heard me crying in the kitchen. He came running in to find me gripping the counter and unable to speak through my tears.

There were no signs of injury. No opened letter. No phone message. All he could do was hold me.

Finally, I was able to sputter, "There's dir—dir—dirty di—di—dishes in the si—si—sink."

Yep—the dishes did me in.

As a young minister, I was certain that "calling" somehow granted me immunity to exhaustion. But my body was sending me a very different message.

Listening to my weary body, perhaps for the first time in my life, I began to see that my life had little to no *margin*. (To be continued.)

FOR REFLECTION AND DISCUSSION

*"Come to me, all you who are weary and
burdened, and I will give you rest."*
(MATTHEW 11:28)

One. Have you ever been close to burnout or breakdown? If so, describe the circumstances that contributed to your exhaustion.

Two. Either from your own experience or from what you have learned from the experiences of close friends, list several ways to safeguard against this degree of debilitating weariness.

Three. Prayerfully respond to Jesus' invitation in Matthew 11:28.

GROW AND GUARD MARGIN

Once I finish the things I *have* to do, I don't have energy left to do the things I *want* to do.

My reserves are depleted. There's nothing left for me to draw on.

It's too much. I don't think I can take any more.

If something doesn't change soon, I'm going to break down or burn out.

Do any of these statements sound or feel familiar?

They certainly are familiar to me. In my exhausted state, I knew I needed help and a meaningful book called *Margin,* by medical doctor Richard Swenson, offered vivid imagery for why change was desperately needed in my life.

Picture a straight horizontal line with three points: A at the beginning, B at about three-quarters of the line, and C at the end.[7]

According to Doctor Swenson, on a normal day God intends us to live between points A and B. The space between points B and C (called margin) is a reserve that we are to store up for crises, for the unexpected, and for the "extra mile."

But in our culture we live between A and C each day. In doing so, we use up that reserve in normal living.

So when a crisis does occur, we have nothing to draw from and we extend ourselves beyond C into overload. When overload is prolonged, it inevitably leads to some kind of burnout.

Looking back over the year of itineration, I realized that I had no margin in my life. I was "spent" every day with nothing saved up for the unexpected.

My husband and I worked together to create a more sane schedule that made room for rest, fun, time at the piano, occasional naps, and the space to simply be blissfully bored.

Growing and guarding margin became a treasured discipline in our lives and family. Even today, I am grateful for its fruit.

FOR REFLECTION AND DISCUSSION

Take my yoke upon you and learn from me, for I am
gentle and humble in heart, and you will find rest for
your souls. For my yoke is easy and my burden is light.
(Matthew 11:29–30)

One. On paper, draw the A B C illustration from the devotional. Does your life have margin? Do you have a reserve built up emotionally? Physically? Spiritually?

Two. If so, what has helped build that reserve? If not, what has been a drain on that reserve?

Three. Jesus states that we can find rest for our souls by taking His yoke and learning from Him. His life changed the world, yet in the Scriptures He never appeared frazzled, fried, or frustrated. We never see Jesus worrying, hurrying, or scurrying. Certainly there were tiring times where He went the extra mile. But He seemed to have sufficient reserves for those days.

Next time you read through the Gospels, consider how Jesus structured His day. In between His timeless teachings, look for patterns in His daily life that contributed to rest and a healthy reserve for crises.

Four. If you are currently in overload or even burnout, ask for the support and prayers of friends and *please* make an appointment with your doctor. Exhaustion can quickly lead to clinical depression and many will affirm that the road back to health from depression can be a painfully long trek.

INVEST IN TUNE-UPS (INSTEAD OF BREAKDOWNS)

"It was probably nothing," I said to Barry, "but the brakes seemed a little sluggish as I pulled into the restaurant." Barry took the wheel on the way home to test the brakes but they performed perfectly. With relief, I dismissed my concerns, assuming it must have just been my imagination.

One week later, we were driving away from campus and had just crested one of Austin's many hills when Barry whispered, "Dear God," and gripped the steering wheel.

Our brakes had completely failed.

Accelerating down the hill during rush hour, Barry thought fast and, rather than rear end the long line of cars waiting at the red light, he veered into the empty oncoming traffic lane in the hope of hitting the intersection when the light turned green.

All I could see were the red tail lights of all the cars we passed as I instinctively, and ineffectively, yelled out of the window, "Our brakes are gone, get out of the way!"

By the grace of God and my husband's level head, we made it to the intersection and Barry cranked the car clipping only one other vehicle before we came to a stop. Thankfully, no one was hurt at all. Well, not physically. To this day, I sometimes still flinch when a car in front of me hits their brakes suddenly.

At first, the policeman, understandably, treated us like thrill-seeking graduate students until the driver of the tow truck tried to move our totaled car. "No brakes," he mouthed, and the policeman immediately softened. It was a miracle that everyone walked away without even a scratch.

I have often looked back on that day at the restaurant.

Why did I not take my concerns more seriously? Yes, I knew little about cars. Yes, it had been raining.

But additionally, I remember being worried about finances.

We were newly married and living on love. But the tune-up would have been much cheaper than the crash, financially and emotionally.

With our vehicles and in our lives, when we too easily dismiss attending to the small things, we will eventually be immobilized by bigger things that are impossible to ignore.

What small things are you ignoring? What little squeaks are you explaining away? What tiny troubles are you hoping to just outrun?

What issues do you need to address while they are still small?

- a stop at the mechanic for the car?

- an appointment with the physical therapist for that ache?

- a consult with a doctor for the weariness?

- a visit with a financial advisor for the budget?

- time with a counselor for the relationship?

- a long talk with a mentor for peace of mind?

Invest in the tune-ups.

In the long run, they are far cheaper than breakdowns.

FOR REFLECTION AND DISCUSSION

Two are better than one,
because they have a good return for their work:
If one falls down,
his friend can help him up.
But pity the man who falls
and has no one to help him up!
(ECCLESIASTES 4:9–10)

One. On a scale of 1 (healthy and strong) to 10 (exhausted and anxious), assess yourself in these areas: physically, emotionally, spiritually, relationally, and financially.

Two. Give yourself some advice. If you heard someone rate the areas in question one as you did, what would you encourage that person to do?

Three. In the words of Jesus, "Go and do likewise." (Luke 10:37) Talk with Father God about any areas you rated 5 – 10, asking Him if they might benefit from wise counsel or professional assistance. For example, "Father, I'm not managing anger well in this situation. Bring to my mind someone who could help me process these recurring emotions."

CHOOSE TO…

HEAR THE INVITATION IN THE STORM

Growing up, whenever thunder would sound in the distance, my dad and I would smile, pause whatever we were doing, and take our places together outside. I have many happy memories of the two of us, sitting side by side in silence, relishing the unpredictable movements of nature's symphonies.

From the beginning, Dad was determined that I, his only child, would not inherit our extended family's fear of storms. "There is nothing to fear," he would say as he scooped me up and carried me outside, where we would watch the storm under the safety of a covered porch.

I still remember… the wind carrying to us the sweet promise of rain, the lightning dancing to a rhythm it alone could hear, and the clouds rolling like an ocean over our heads.

While the storm proclaimed nature's untamed power, I sat in perfect peace tucked under Dad's arm, and tears of contentment would collect in my young eyes.

Over the decades, I grew to savor storms: they were an invitation to rest with my daddy.

Dad's arms can no longer hold me. I am reminded of that reality every time I hear a distant thunder. But Another still sits near me when the winds beat against my life.

> Life's storms are rather impolite.
>
> They neither consult our calendars nor consider our hearts.
>
> Without requesting permission, they simply come.

But each time they come, I believe that Father God whispers to our spirits, "I am here. There is nothing to fear."

When the earth shakes and dreams crumble, God's strong arms are open to us. When winds howl and faith trembles, God offers to hide us in Himself.

Life's storms issue to us an invitation to rest with God.

Nestled securely in His embrace, His love faithfully accompanies us through even the most furious of storms.

FOR REFLECTION AND DISCUSSION

> *[Jesus] got up and rebuked the winds and the waves, and it was completely calm. The men were amazed and asked, "What kind of man is this? Even the winds and the waves obey him!"*
> (MATTHEW 8:26–27)

One. If life's storms are currently sweeping across the landscape of your heart, make a concerted effort today to sit alone with God for a few moments. Forego trusting in your own strength and picture yourself nestled within His strong arms. Grant yourself permission to be weak in His presence.

Two. In that sweet space of dependence, meditate on this Scripture prayer based on Psalm 91:1–4, 14–15:

> I choose to dwell in Your shelter, Most High God.
> I rest in Your almighty shadow.
> You are my refuge and my fortress.
> You are my God and I trust You.
> You will save me from the enemy's schemes and attacks.
> You cover me with Your feathers.
> Under Your wings I find refuge.
> Your faithfulness is my shield;
> I will not be afraid.
> I love You, Lord.
> I believe You will rescue me and protect me.
> I call on You today and I know You will answer me.
> You are with me in this time of trouble.
> I wait for Your deliverance.

Three. One of the healthiest choices we can make when we are overwhelmed with life's storms is to intentionally offer prayers for others who are also in crisis. Consider the tremendous needs of others today. Pray Psalm 91 over their lives asking God to be the dwelling place of the homeless, to provide rest for the broken, and to be a fortress for the forgotten.

NAME YOUR REAL FEAR

Ours is a fun and fabulous story.

I met Barry at a university ministry's retreat. Our interest in one another grew over a piano and a ping pong table. We courted via snail mail and phone calls across the Pacific. Barry sold his motorcycle (yes, that is love) to buy a plane ticket to Australia (where I was serving as a campus minister) and propose to me.

And then I hit a wall.

Many friends and family members had already purchased plane tickets to our wedding when I announced that it was postponed "indefinitely."

All had been moving along rather well until a few months before the wedding date when we learned that an esteemed leader—whom we both admired—had an affair. All who heard were shocked by the news.

In the weeks that followed, I watched helplessly from across the ocean as the ensuing chaos shattered a community. Each new revelation hung over me like a thickening cloud and something began to gather in the shadows.

Barry wept and prayed over the news. But my grief was extreme: I was shaken to my very core. Of course the situation was grievous. But the depth to which it affected me was beyond the bounds of reason. I was paralyzed.

"Are you okay?" Barry would ask.

"I don't know," I would reply.

Something was shifting within me.

And that shift began to affect our relationship.

I found myself more easily irritated with Barry, more impatient, and definitely more critical. I questioned the veracity of our love. Unconsciously, I was withdrawing my emotional investment, bowing to an oppressive yet unnamed substance growing in my soul.

The wedding was off. A time of fasting had begun.

Returning home from Australia, I spent uncounted hours on my face in prayer, eventually identifying that nameless substance as *fear*.

That revelation was helpful, but more work was needed.

Unidentified, fear is oppressive: it casts vague and heavy shadows over our thoughts.

Identified but still unnamed, fear is possessive: it refuses to release its grip on our hearts.

Yes, I was afraid. But of what?

With the wedding called off, my life was graced with much needed space. My church kindly opened an unused room to me and I spent the next two months in prayer. It felt like there was a knot of fear in my soul, as though a cat had toyed with a ball of yarn for years. The tangle was beyond me, but not beyond my Mentor.

> *God, what is it that I'm really afraid of?*

Through cycles of worship, reading the Word, and waiting, fear's specific name revealed itself.

> *Lord, if a leader like this man of God can fall, anyone can. What if unfaithfulness touches our love? Oh God, I think I'd rather never love than try to survive failed love.*

I was afraid of failure.

FOR REFLECTION AND DISCUSSION

> *Let love and faithfulness never leave you;*
> *bind them around your neck,*
> *write them on the tablet of your heart.*
> (PROVERBS 3:3)

One. Barry refers to the season in which I received the sad news about the leader as "dark December." Dark it was! At the time, I had no idea that the freon chilling my veins was called fear. How vulnerable do you feel you are to fear?

Two. What are your fears most often focused upon? For example, finances? Loved ones? Health? Global crisis?

Three. It is easy to believe that if Jesus were physically beside us, we would not be afraid. Yet, even those within arm's reach of Jesus experienced paralyzing fear (see Mark 4:35–41). What do you think truly helps someone build up immunity to the tyranny of fear?

CHOOSE TO...

RENOUNCE UNHOLY ALLIANCES

Another revelation that awaited me in that simple prayer room regarded the roots and fruits of my fear of failure.

As for fruits, when afraid of failure, I became more critical and controlling in an attempt to avoid what I feared. This was a miserable reality for Barry. I analyzed and critiqued him, subconsciously searching for a reason to excuse myself from loving him.

In those dark months, Barry tenaciously held on to God while God tenaciously held on to me and sowed life-giving principles in my soul.

Returning daily to my little room of prayer at church, I began to realize that I would never be free *from* fear if I kept willfully strengthening my alliance *with* fear.

Fear is a master of disguises.

She clothes herself as *caution*, and we sit at her feet.

She introduces herself as *wisdom*, and we listen to her, unguarded.

She presents herself as *just being prepared*, and we invite her to help us plan for the future.

As the clouds began to clear, it became painfully obvious that I had formed an unholy alliance with fear.

I thought with fear and planned with fear.

I asked fear to counsel me so I could avoid problems and stay one step ahead of pain.

I requested fear to advise me so that disappointments would not catch me by surprise and disasters would not find me unprepared.

The esteemed leader's failure had recently thrown oil on the fire of my fear but I had been willfully tending that old flame for years.

In my daily life, in big and small ways, I had developed a habit of honoring fear like a holy helper. I had aligned myself with fear like a trusted friend.

How?

By investing enormous amounts of mental energy entertaining *what could possibly go wrong* scenarios and preparing for them as though they were inevitable.

If at this point, you are shrugging your shoulders and thinking, "What on earth is Alicia talking about?" please feel free to skip the next chapter and continue with the book. But if you are thinking, "Dear God, this is where I live!" consider the following verses carefully:

The fear of the Lord is pure, enduring forever. (Psalm 19:9)

Blessed is the man who fears the Lord,
who finds great delight in his commands.... .
He will have no fear of bad news;
his heart is steadfast, trusting in the Lord.
His heart is secure, he will have no fear. (Psalm 112:1, 7–8)

God did not give us a spirit of timidity [i.e., fearful
apprehension], but a spirit of power, of love and of
self-discipline. (2 Timothy 1:7)

In examining my fear through the lens of Scripture, its toxic fruits were
vividly exposed: my fear of failure was not pure, I did fear bad news,
my heart was not at peace, and my mind was apprehensive. I lived on
alert: ever vigilant to protect myself from, and prepare myself to avoid,
potential pain.

This was not the fear of God.

This was the fear of failure.

And its roots were in an unholy alliance that had to be
rejected and renounced.

This was a key turning point for me spiritually. I still remember kneeling
on the worn carpet and, in Jesus' name with a simple prayer, cancelling
my contract with fear.

The relief was tangible.

So after that monumental day of prayer, was I ever tempted to renew
that unholy alliance and sit at fear's feet in a vain attempt to avoid pain?

Yes, indeed.

Marriage, ministry, publishing, and especially parenthood have all provided numerous opportunities for me to reaffirm the choice I made so many years ago.

Renouncing my unholy alliance with fear had revoked its hidden power in my life and placed me safely on God's side in the battle.

Through His Word and by His grace, I continue to grow stronger in the fight.

FOR REFLECTION AND DISCUSSION

Preserve sound judgment and discernment,
do not let them out of your sight;
they will be life for you,
an ornament to grace your neck.
Then you will go on your way in safety,
and your foot will not stumble;
when you lie down, you will not be afraid;
when you lie down, your sleep will be sweet.
Have no fear of sudden disaster
or of the ruin that overtakes the wicked,
for the Lord will be your confidence
and will keep your foot from being snared.
(PROVERBS 3:21–26)

One. When gripped by the fear of failure, I became more critical and controlling. How do you respond when afraid? What does fear produce in you?

Two. Have you ever formed an alliance with fear? Have you thought with fear or asked fear to counsel you in an attempt to stay one step ahead of pain, problems, or crises? If the message of this devotional resonates with you, please carve out several minutes to respond in prayer. Read Proverbs 3:21-26 aloud and, in Jesus' name, break all alliances with fear.

Three. Personally, whenever I am tempted to sit at fear's feet, I actively engage my mind in something spiritually beneficial. Below I offer a list of personal strategies to fight fear. Feel free to edit this list into whatever will help you "preserve sound judgment and discernment" next time fear comes calling.

- Pray for others in need.

- Memorize Scripture.

- Pray Scripture over situations.

- Open the Bible and read out loud.

- Use your imagination to picture a relevant story from the Bible, like Jesus calming the storm or the angel being sent to shut the lions' mouths for Daniel.

SEEK WHAT PLEASES GOD

After repenting of trusting in fear (more than God) as my guide, a sweet freedom washed over me and I was filled with joy.

I wanted to find a phone and call Barry with the news. Surely we could move forward now!

Father God was, no doubt, smiling. Fear of failure was the loudest—but not the only—hindrance to love in my heart that He planned to address.

He had yet another life-giving principle to plant in my soul that would be a guide in my understanding of His will for decades to come:

> It is inconsistent with His character for Him to be pleased by something that would draw me away from Him.

Allow me to explain.

As a single person, I felt conflicted about marriage. On one hand, I longed to share life with someone who loved God wholeheartedly. On the other hand, I feared that marriage would distract me from nearness with God. As a former Atheist, my relationship with Jesus was priceless and I was willing to take whatever path might be best for me personally to keep that relationship flourishing.

In the Scriptures, I saw examples of God's blessing on both marriage and singleness. Clearly, He brought people together and clearly, He at times called some not to marry. What was He calling me toward?

The question contained three critical components in my mind: marriage itself, marriage to Barry specifically, and marriage at that time of my life. The combination made my brain hurt.

So I kept spilling out my heart to God in prayer. Our conversation went something like this:

> *"Father God, will marrying Barry draw me closer to You? I know that Barry loves You, but does that mean that we will both love You more together?"*

"Alicia, it pleases Me for you to marry Barry."

> *"Yes, thanks. BUT will marriage draw me closer to You?"*

"It pleases Me for you to marry Barry," He repeated.

And then it dawned on me: it is inconsistent with God's character for Him to be pleased by something that draws me away from Him. His pleasure was His approval.

Now, no doubt, there would still be work to do and aches to navigate. A brief glance at the life of Mary, the mother of Jesus, makes it obvious that being led by God's pleasure does not grant us immunity to pain.

But I was not afraid of difficulties. I just wanted to protect First Love.

The longer I lingered in prayer, the deeper God's pleasure settled into my soul. Through waiting, I emerged from that season of prayer confident that for me, marrying Barry pleased the heart of God.

God's character makes God's pleasure a trustworthy guide.

FOR REFLECTION AND DISCUSSION

"For I know the plans I have for you," declares the Lord, "plans to prosper you and not to harm you, plans to give you hope and a future. Then you will call upon me and come and pray to me, and I will listen to you. You will seek me and find me when you seek me with all your heart."
(JEREMIAH 29:11–13)

One. "How can I know God's will?" is perhaps among the most frequently asked questions of every generation. Write down some areas in which you are currently seeking to know God's will. Select one to prayerfully consider for the remaining reflection prompts.

Two. The first source to consult when we are seeking God's will is the Bible. Are there any stories or principles from Scripture that might be relevant to the decisions you are facing? For example, the Bible obviously does not contain a prophecy that says, "In 1990 Alicia will marry Barry." But the Scriptures do identify the qualities of a godly leader, all of which are relevant when screening a potential spouse.

Three. God has also graciously given us brains. If the Scriptures have not settled the issue, engage your grey matter further by, for example, listing pros and cons and listening to the advice of those you trust. Take a few minutes to write down the names of those whom you would trust to give godly advice if you were facing a major decision.

Four. Having consulted God's Word, engaged your brain, and considered the advice of trusted leaders, read Jeremiah 29:11–13 again and take the wisdom you have collected into a time of prayer. Thank God that His plans for you are good and recommit to seeking whatever would please Him.

CHOOSE TO…

PAY THE PRICE FOR GREATER INTIMACY

For each life, there is a path called obedience.

It always leads to greater intimacy with God.

And greater intimacy with God often requires greater intentionality.

This was among the many surprising lessons awaiting me as a newlywed.

As you have read in previous chapters, "dark December" was followed by months of prayer and healing for me. Then one summer day, Barry and I said our vows in full assurance that our covenant would be blessed by the pleasure of God.

What I did not realize is that drawing closer to God as a couple would not be automatic.

What? I thought after the first few weeks. *Why didn't anyone prepare me for this? Shouldn't this be a topic of discussion in premarital counseling?*

I would start to worship… and someone would JOIN IN.

I would be meditating on Scripture… and someone would ASK ME A QUESTION.

I would be waiting on God in silence… and someone would START WHISTLING.

Poor Barry. This introverted, only child he had married had a lot of learning to do.

My husband loved God with all of his heart. But the consistent presence of someone else in my space was cramping my devotional style.

Gone were the days of just my Bible, my journal, and Jesus.

Gone were the days of complete solitude.

Gone were the nights of glorious silence. (Barry snored, and—who knew??—so did I!)

Now someone was *near me* when I was *near God.*

To some, this probably sounds ridiculous. But many souls have shared with me how surprised they were that, initially, marriage almost seemed a distraction from intimacy with God.

For a few, the challenge was adjusting to drastically decreased solitude. For some, it was hard to carve out time to read the Word when they would rather be relaxing with their spouse. For others, they were so thrilled to finally have a human to talk with that they found themselves talking to God less.

And this challenge is not limited to marriage. The same frustrations can be experienced when we are getting used to a new roommate, taking care of an aging parent, moving from the countryside to the city, or transitioning to a more relational work environment.

Greater intimacy often requires greater intentionality.

Over the years, greater intentionality for me has included an expanded understanding of worship, increased communication with my family, flexibility with schedules, constant creativity in the use of time, and incorporating the practice of monthly prayer retreats.

Where has the path of obedience led you?

Whether into this ministry or that marketplace, into being single or being married, into being an uncle or being a daddy, that path *will* lead to greater intimacy with God.

(And it may require greater intentionality to get there.)

FOR REFLECTION AND DISCUSSION

This is love for God: to obey his commands.
(1 John 5:3)

One. Describe any transitions or experiences that have disrupted the flow of your devotional life.

Two. "For each life, there is a path called obedience. It always leads to greater intimacy with God and greater intimacy with God will often require greater intentionality." Rephrase this principle in your own words.

Three. Perhaps with the help of friends, brainstorm creative ways to become more disciplined in your pursuit of greater intimacy with God. Personally, I have to reassess my devotional life every few months to keep it fresh and growing.

CHOOSE TO...

DEFINE FAITHFULNESS BIBLICALLY

Have you ever felt confused about God's faithfulness?

> God is faithful... but His servants still know pain. (Consider Stephen who was stoned for speaking truth in Acts 7:59.)

> God is faithful... but His followers experience depression. (Consider the great prophet Elijah who prayed that he might die in 1 Kings 19:4.)

> God is faithful... but those who love Him are familiar with loss. (Consider the prophetess Anna who was barren and widowed at a young age as recounted in Luke 2:36–37.)

> God is faithful... but His people endure injustice. (Consider Joseph who was sold into slavery by his jealous older brothers in Genesis 37:28.)

Is God truly faithful if His people suffer in this life?

In both the Old and New Testaments, the words used to describe God's faithfulness carry the meaning of *truth*, *believability*, and *assurance*.

The writers of the Bible—who knew trouble and hardship in this world firsthand—unanimously confirm that God can be trusted, relied on, and believed in: He is a faithful God.

> Moses proclaimed, "The Lord your God is God; he is the faithful God, keeping his covenant of love to a thousand generations of those who love him and keep his commands…. a faithful God who does no wrong, upright and just is he." (Deuteronomy 7:9 and 32:4)

> David asserted, "All the ways of the Lord are loving and faithful for those who keep the demands of his covenant…. he is faithful in all he does." (Psalm 25:10 and 33:4)

> Jeremiah declared, "Because of the Lord's great love we are not consumed, for his compassions never fail. They are new every morning; great is your faithfulness." (Lamentations 3:22–23)

> Paul taught, "God, who has called you into fellowship with his Son Jesus Christ our Lord, is faithful." (1 Corinthians 1:9)

> Peter counseled, "Those who suffer according to God's will should commit themselves to their faithful Creator and continue to do good." (1 Peter 4:19)

> And John affirmed that Jesus "is faithful and just." (1 John 1:9)

These same writers understood rejection, betrayal, wars, difficult living conditions, the loss of children, and family strife. They were well acquainted with homelessness, false accusations, rejection, and emotional deserts. They knew sickness, deep discouragement, failure, bitter conflict, and persecution.

> From their perspective, suffering did not invalidate God's faithfulness.

> Suffering is where they experienced God's faithfulness.

Perhaps our confusion comes from a belief that the purpose of God's faithfulness is to protect us from pain, shield us from harm, and keep us from disappointment.

But the writers of the Bible saw evidence of God's faithfulness not in their comfort level or circumstances but in God's constant companionship: He was with them *in* the trials, fires, and aches of life.

> God's faithfulness is not a passport out of trouble in this world.

> God's faithfulness is a promise of His presence in this world and in the world to come!

The faithfulness of God does not exist to keep us free from pain but to keep us focused on the path toward heaven.

God has an eternal agenda: to faithfully guide our souls—through the suffering and joy, loss and gain, conflict and peace—into His everlasting arms.

So, as the writer of Hebrews encouraged:

> Let us draw near to God with a sincere heart in full assurance of faith, having our hearts sprinkled to cleanse us

from a guilty conscience and having our bodies washed with pure water. Let us hold unswervingly to the hope we profess, for he who promised is faithful. (Hebrews 10:22–23)

FOR REFLECTION AND DISCUSSION

Here is a trustworthy saying: If we died with him, we will also live with him; if we endure, we will also reign with him. If we disown him, he will also disown us; if we are faithless, he will remain faithful, for he cannot disown himself.
(2 TIMOTHY 2:11–13)

One. Throughout the Scriptures, those who frequently spoke of God's faithfulness were extremely familiar with suffering. How does our modern understanding of faithfulness contrast with the biblical understanding of faithfulness?

Two. "Suffering did not invalidate God's faithfulness. Suffering is where they experienced God's faithfulness." Recall a time when you knew God's faithfulness in the midst of suffering. What did that experience grow in you?

Three. Consider the truth that God is preparing you, not just for tomorrow, but for eternity. Journal any thoughts and discoveries.

Four: You may have noticed that this is the only devotional that lacks a story. For this chapter, you will supply the story by filling in a few blanks:

(*your name*) knew (*list trials you have experienced*) and still proclaimed that God was (*list what you know to be true about God*).

CHOOSE TO...

OFFER THE ACHE TO GOD

As a special needs family, schooling was, and still is, a regular topic of concern. Every year (and sometimes every semester) we would seek God's wisdom for what context would be best for our children. Homeschool? Private school? Public school? Specialized tutors?

Though we are grateful for the extraordinary teachers and tutors who have been a part of our village over the years, our annual decision-making about schooling was less about academics and more about the kids' spiritual, emotional, and social well-being.

Our rural public school was a wonderful all-around fit for our eldest up until the third grade. That is when the peer-pain led us to a private school and ultimately homeschool and tutoring until he graduated from high school and went on to college.

The story below was written when Jonathan was nine about his first day in third grade. I have left it in the present tense to preserve the ache. It is an ache I know some of you share daily.

My son cried today.

Walking into school, bigger children began to pour cruel words on him.

Though I intervened, their few words penetrated his mind like poisonous darts.

My precious child fell to the floor and buried his head in the carpet. This mother's heart was ripped apart. I would do anything to shield him from such pain.

Rejection is surely one of the most devastating wounds humanity inflicts on itself.

My ache only expands as I consider the rejection that may shadow my special son.

His amazing mind sees the world in an unusual way. That gift makes him strong because it enables him to offer a unique contribution to this world for God. But that gift also makes him vulnerable because he is different.

Later during cuddle time, Jonathan whispered to me through his pain.

"Mom, I'm really different. Like when I laugh, no one else does. I wish, I wish—"

"Yes, love?"

"I'm too shy to say it."

"Do you wish you weren't different?"

(silence)

In the light of the moon, I shared with Jonathan how different I always felt while growing up: the last kid picked for teams, the first kid others made fun of. I, too, have always seen the world in a different way. "Your difference is a gift," I assured him, "but it may take a long time for others to see and value that gift."

Staring into eyes that seemed too wise for his age, I told my son that Jesus was also very different and that people often hurt Him with their words. "My love," I offered, "since Jesus knows the pain of rejection, He can help us forgive others when they reject us."

Jonathan paused thoughtfully for a moment. Then, softly shaking his head, he said, "Okay, Mom," as he gave me a big bear hug.

Listening to his breathing as he fell asleep, I reflected on the pain of childhood peer rejection.

I contemplated the challenges my son was currently facing.

And I realized that I was crying.

FOR REFLECTION AND DISCUSSION

The Lord is close to the brokenhearted
and saves those who are crushed in spirit.
(Psalm 34:18)

One. Peer rejection was so pervasive in my childhood that it actually contributed to a depression where I considered suicide in my early teens. Rejection is a powerful and persuasive force. How familiar were you with rejection as a child? As an adult?

Two. During another teachable moment, I shared with Jonathan that people often say mean things because they have bruises in their hearts. But letting mean words stick to you is like stepping on gum and then choosing not to remove it from your shoe: it can make you feel off-balance and it causes dirt to stick to your soul. (No pun intended.) Take an honest inventory of your heart. Is any "gum" sticking to your soul? In prayer, place wounding words and experiences that are haunting you in Jesus' pierced hands.

Three. Close with a prayer of protection for the hearts, minds, and spirits of the children in your life.

LEAVE A LEGACY OF LOVE

Like a gluttonous guest who arrived uninvited, cancer ate away at my friend's life. Nibble by nibble, bite by bite, the disease shaved off the edges of her future.

Holding her hand, I was overwhelmed by the change. The tumor was growing rapidly. She could no longer walk or move. I was not sure if I would ever hear her speak again.

Questions stirred restlessly in my soul:

What about her children? What about her husband? God, please do something!

Few love life like she does. Few love people like she does.

Why, God?

Where are the healings Jesus' voice brought to so many when He walked on this earth?

Unoffended by my questioning, God gently brought His words to my memory:

> "Are not two sparrows sold for a penny? Yet not one of them will fall to the ground apart from the will of your Father. And even the very hairs of your head are all numbered. So don't be afraid." (Matthew 10:29–31)

> Precious in the sight of the Lord is the death of his saints. (Psalm 116:15)

> Who shall separate us from the love of Christ? Shall trouble or hardship or persecution or famine or nakedness or danger or sword?… I am convinced that neither death nor life, neither angels nor demons, neither the present nor the future, not any powers, neither height nor depth, nor anything else in all creation, will be able to separate us from the love of God that is in Christ Jesus our Lord. (Romans 8:35, 38–39)

Truth stabilized my answer-less heart.

Suffering might steal my friend's strength, but no force in heaven or hell could steal the love of God from her life.

Then suddenly she opened her eyes and looked into mine!

Smiling slightly, she slowly formed the last words I ever heard her say. With her gentle southern accent she whispered, "L-luv (pause) you."

Nearing the end of her life, what did she want me to know? What she had accomplished? What she regretted? What others should have done or not done to her?

No. There was only one message she wanted to relay: she wanted me to know that I was loved.

Her peace, and her love, passed understanding.

Truly, God's love in and through her was stronger than life.

FOR REFLECTION AND DISCUSSION

I am always with you;
you hold me by my right hand.
You guide me with your counsel,
and afterward you will take me into glory.
Whom have I in heaven but you?
And earth has nothing I desire besides you.
My flesh and my heart may fail,
but God is the strength of my heart
and my portion forever.
(Psalm 73:23–26)

One. Take a few moments to remember loved ones who have died. Thank God specifically for each one, remembering their unique contributions to your life.

Two. Write down before God any questions you have about their suffering or deaths.

Three. Though we all hope that long life is before us, whom would you want to remind that they are loved if your days were shortened? What actions can you take to begin leaving that legacy of love now?

Four. Conclude by Scripture-praying some of this devotional's verses over the lives of those who are currently suffering. For example, "You, O God, have numbered the hairs on Joe's head. Strengthen him today not to be afraid."

APPLAUD OBEDIENCE

The large auditorium was filled to capacity.

Corporate worship filled the air with anticipation.

The speaker's message was stirring.

And then as he closed, he gave a singular challenge to the thousands of students gathered that day: "If you sense God's call into full-time ministry, please stand!"

The room exploded in approving applause as perhaps one hundred teens stood with tears in their eyes.

I held my breath and waited.

And then my eyes filled with tears too, not for those who stood, but for the teens who were still seated, the adults that were still applauding, and the lost who are still waiting.

Why? Because I had hoped to hear other calls.

Calls like…

> "If you sense God's call to minister as educators, please stand!"

> "If you feel God planting you in politics, please stand!"

> "If you are being directed by God to serve Him through the arts, please stand!"

But there were no other calls. There was no other applause.

As I closed my eyes, I wondered what we had just communicated to those teens who remained seated because we only issued one call.

What must they have felt when, in integrity before Jesus, they knew the minister was not calling, and the church was not applauding, for people like them?

How easy it is for us as a church to applaud "the ministry" over other professions.

How easy it is to give more honor and attribute more value to those with certain titles and roles.

> Unlike us, Jesus does not applaud position.

> He applauds obedience.

His favor, delight, and power rest equally on all who follow Him in obedience, regardless of whether obedience leads us to local neighborhoods or distant lands, to public schools or to pulpits.

Without question, God calls some to minister in traditional roles. As Paul stated,

> Christ himself gave the apostles, the prophets, the evangelists, the pastors and teachers, to equip his people for works of service, so that the body of Christ may be built up until we all reach unity in the faith and in the knowledge of the Son of God and become mature, attaining to the whole measure of the fullness of Christ. (Ephesians 4:11–13)

And God also gifts His people with expertise in arts and crafts as we see in the building of the temple in the Old Testament (see Exodus 31:1–5) and the many skills that are affirmed in the New Testament from tentmaking (see Acts 18:3) to textiles (see Acts 16:14).

Our *primary* call is to follow Jesus. That "follow" leads some to serve God as accountants, actors, athletes, carpenters, coaches, computer scientists, lawyers, nurses, plumbers, teachers, and hundreds of other occupations.

I believe that limiting our definition of "ministry" to the activity of professional clergy is like leaving the vast portion of a rich gold mine untouched.

Jesus commissioned all who followed Him to be His witnesses "to the ends of the earth." (Acts 1:8) Fulfilling that Great Commission will require a world-size commitment from us all.

Together, with honor for all the giftings and callings God has given His people, we can be ambassadors of love to our generation until the whole world knows of God's love!

FOR REFLECTION AND DISCUSSION

> *Therefore, if anyone is in Christ, he is a new creation; the*
> *old has gone, the new has come! All this is from God, who*
> *reconciled us to himself through Christ and gave us the ministry*
> *of reconciliation.... We are therefore Christ's ambassadors,*
> *as though God were making his appeal through us.*
>
> (2 Corinthians 5:17–18, 20)

> *There are different kinds of gifts, but the same Spirit*
> *distributes them. There are different kinds of service, but*
> *the same Lord. There are different kinds of working, but in*
> *all of them and in everyone it is the same God at work.*
>
> (1 Corinthians 12:4–6)

One. How do you view the following activities? Are they ministry? Why or why not?

- pastoring a church
- parenting
- lecturing at a Bible school
- lecturing at a university
- caring for an abandoned child at an overseas orphanage
- caring for a foster child locally
- teaching missionary children in Brazil
- teaching public school children in Florida
- being an accountant for a church
- being an accountant for a company
- serving as a counselor at a youth camp
- serving as a coach for a city soccer team

Two. Consider your calling to partner with God in His great love for the world. List below any skills you have that cannot be used to serve God and others.

_____

_____

_____

Three. Evidently all other skills can be used! Think about the abilities God has given you. Prayerfully conclude with a focus on ministry to those near you. Wait on God for creative ways in which you can serve them today and remind yourself that in serving them in Jesus' name, you are faithfully participating in God's great mission.[8]

CHOOSE TO...

REJOICE

Vaulted ceilings have always been attractive to me. I find their openness inspiring.

So when we were building my office above the garage, I asked the contractor to give me every inch of height that he could. He smiled and pushed my multi-angled ceiling as close to the roof line as possible. No doubt, it was a lot more work for him, but he had one very happy customer when the job was done.

Perhaps only a few share my love for high ceilings. But my guess is that almost all share a discomfort with low ceilings, whether physical or interpersonal.

In politics, academia, business, medicine, and even the church, more than a few have experienced frustration over low ceilings or, even more exasperating, undisclosed glass ceilings—invisible yet real barriers to opportunity or advancement.

When such ceilings are shattered, all who dream of greater liberty rejoice.

Well, my friend, you have reason to rejoice! There is no glass ceiling between you and God. A splintered cross shattered it long ago!

Jesus endured the cruelty of crucifixion to pay for your sins with His death. Through His sacrifice, Father God holds a high opinion of you, His forgiven one.

Rejoice! The ceiling separating you from God has been dismantled by love!

> No circumstance can doom you to a stale, stagnant spirituality.

> No season can limit you to an out-of-date, out-of-breath faith.

Rejoice: The ceiling of separation has been broken. Intimacy with God is attainable!

> Lift up your head.

> Stand tall.

> Reach high.

God's great desire is for you to know Him both now and forevermore!

FOR REFLECTION AND DISCUSSION

But you are a chosen people, a royal priesthood, a holy nation, a people belonging to God, that you may declare the praises of him who called you out of darkness into his wonderful light.

(1 PETER 2:9)

One. In God's presence, ask yourself if you have ever felt that there was a glass ceiling to the intimacy you could experience with Him. This sense of spiritual limitation can arise from remorse over past failures, stress over pressing matters, helplessness over others' choices, or even doubts about our ability or God's character.

Two. Often a sense of discontentment arises from a belief that we are "stuck," that something we long for is unattainable because of our current circumstances. While this may be true academically or even professionally, this is never true spiritually. This season of life is as rich with possibilities for intimacy with God as any ever has been and any ever will be. Turn to God in prayer and ask Him to open your eyes to this season's spiritual potential.

Three. In Romans 8:39, Paul declared that nothing "can separate us from the love of God." Truly, because of Jesus' sacrifice, there are no barriers to intimacy with God. Conclude your time of reflection with thanksgiving to God for the spiritual potential of today.

CELEBRATE WHAT IS NEAR

How long had I been staring out the window? Sitting in my writing chair one winter morning my thoughts had been wandering over far off hills while hot tea warmed my hands.

Then, a slight movement caught my attention, causing me to refocus closer in. There, I was delighted to see at least three dozen birds just outside the window busily pecking at the frozen earth.

Gathering food, their movements lacked any discernible choreography. The disorderly dance brought a smile to my face as I began to wonder, *How long have they been here?*

A minute? Half an hour? Perhaps the entire time?

Whatever the time frame, something delightful had almost completely escaped my notice.

> I was too distracted gazing over the distant horizon to look straight down.

I was looking for inspiration from afar not nearby.

And then—in the time it took to form that simple thought—every single one of those birds flew off to grace another space.

(I hope they were noticed more quickly there.)

Many years ago, I heard an eloquent speaker challenge a group of leaders to, "Focus your vision on what is small not big; what is near not far."[9]

The words took many by surprise. I could almost see the thought bubbles of confusion popping up over the host of visionary leaders:

> *What? Did I just hear him say to focus on "small" and "near"? Being a leader is about dreaming big, right? Isn't faith about seeing what can't be seen?*

Though it does take faith to see what cannot be seen (see Hebrews 11:1), it also takes faith to follow Jesus in what *can* be seen, i.e., the here and now. These two applications of faith are not in tension. They just represent different dimensions of what it means to walk by faith.

In my culture, the former tends to be more emphasized than the latter.

We are taught to motivate ourselves by reaching for what is currently beyond our reach; to set our sights on a future dream and use today, like a stepping stone, to work toward it.

Dreaming is certainly a God-given ability. But its purpose is to increase, not decrease, our respect for the potential of what is right here, right now.

Yet sometimes we become so forward-thinking that we begin to believe that only tomorrow's accomplishments can give today meaning.

We live as though this moment will only become valuable *retroactively*.

Untrue.

Even if tomorrow never arrives, today is a treasure. There are birds by the dozens gathered on the trees of today. But we will miss them if our eyes are only fixed on the hills beyond the horizon.

> Life is abundant right now.
>
> Life is worthy of being celebrated right here.
>
> Life in this moment is glorious.

May God grant us eyes of faith to see—not only *what will be* one day—but *what already is* right now.

And may we join Him in seeing each bird come in, one by one . .

FOR REFLECTION AND DISCUSSION

"Look at the birds of the air..."
(MATTHEW 6:26)

One. Do you naturally look for inspiration from what is small or big? Near or far?

Two. If possible, take a moment to look outside and journal about what you see. How can that which is nearby inspire you today?

Three. Over the next few days, make a conscious effort to notice life on the ground. Carry your journal with you to document other's quotes, loved ones' quirks, and nature's movements.

Four. Determine this week to celebrate the small and take pleasure in what God has placed within your arm's reach.

ASK BOLDLY

One day, my daughter's words transported me into Bible times. To be specific, I felt like I was listening in on Jesus' conversation with the Canaanite woman who asked Him to have mercy on her and heal her troubled daughter:

> He answered, "I was sent only to the lost sheep of Israel…. It is not right to take the children's bread and toss it to their dogs." "Yes, Lord," she said, "but even the dogs eat the crumbs that fall from their masters' table." Then Jesus answered, "Woman, you have great faith!" (Matthew 15:24–28)

Though I had heard several thoughtful sermons about this passage and had studied it personally, Jesus' interaction with this desperate soul was hard for me to process… until my daughter helped me.

My youngest has always been a rather selective eater. Exposed to meth in the womb, he struggled with various sensitivities especially to touch, taste, and texture.

When he was twelve months old, his favorite "food" was a cheesy snack stick made by a company that, for the price they charged for sixteen sticks in a cute container, surely based their headquarters on a cruise ship.

ANYWAY…

These were Louie's special treats. They were made in a way that was easy for him to break down with his tiny teeth and sensitive gums.

The rest of us had a wide variety of foods we could enjoy, but Louie's choices at that time were very limited. My precious Keona understood this well.

So one day, when I was feeding Louie, Keona asked, "Mommy, I know these are for Louie, but can I have the leftovers from Louie's snack if he throws them on the floor?"

There in my kitchen, I suddenly saw the Canaanite woman acknowledging that Jesus' earthly ministry was in many ways customized for the Jewish people. I saw her quietly but confidently asking for the "leftovers" to be made available for her, a Gentile.

Keona knew that I would give her anything in the fridge. She did not want to take Louie's food because she knew it was made especially for him. But if he discarded it, if he did not need or want it—could she feast on what he refused?

What did I do when faced with such a sensitive, wise, and unashamed request? I opened the can and offered her all 16 of those cheesy treats!

And years later, I am still thinking about what all that means for me, a Gentile sinner saved by grace.

FOR REFLECTION AND DISCUSSION

"Woman, you have great faith! Your request is granted."
(MATTHEW 15:28)

One. I doubt that this Canaanite mother thought of herself as possessing "great faith." She simply loved her daughter and was desperate for help. Such love and desperation gave her a humble yet bold spirit. What prayers do you desperately need God to answer?

Two. Consider Hebrews 10:19–23 and remind yourself that through Jesus you have access to God's throne room in prayer.

Three. Conclude your time by boldly bringing before Father God the prayer needs that weigh most heavily on your heart.

CHOOSE TO...

SAY YEA

Naysayers.

Every season of life is "graced" with them.

When I broke an engagement in college because I did not have peace about getting married, the naysayers said, "Too bad. Good men are hard to come by."

(I have been married to a very, very good man for a very, very long time.)

When I graduated from college and went overseas to serve in the Far East, the naysayers said, "Too dangerous. You'll get sick."

(I came home healthy and happy.)

When newly married, the naysayers told me, "If you make it through the first year, you might be okay."

(The first year was glorious.)

Then they said, "Yeah, but watch out for the seventh year… and for the fifteenth year…"

(The seventh year was rich and the fifteenth year was radiant.)

When I became a mother through the miracle of adoption, the naysayers said, "Congratulations, BUT—you might as well put ministry on hold for a few decades."

(My parenting years have been among the most fruitful ministry years of my life.)

When our kids were little, the naysayers foretold, "Smile now—the terrible twos are coming for that one," or "You say they're a joy, but wait until they become teenagers."

(I have treasured every month and year of my children's lives.)

And, to date, I still wonder why some feel the need to say "nay" in the face of happiness.

> Perhaps they feel a burden to warn others of what might happen.

> Perhaps they project their own fears on others' realities.

> Perhaps they assume that the challenges they encountered are a given for all.

Whatever the root, I find the fruit unpleasant.

Yes, I ached to be married after I broke the engagement. But God sowed spiritual intimacy in the soil of that loneliness.

Yes, I had my share of East-meets-West stomach viruses traveling overseas. But God sowed dependence in the soil of my weakness.

Yes, good marriages require constant attention. But God sowed character in the soil of mutual commitment.

Yes, as a special needs mom, I chose to travel less. But God sowed wondrous adventure in the soil of life-together.

Perhaps the difference between being a naysayer and being a yea-sayer is *focus*.

> The focus of a naysayer is to avoid trouble, weakness, or pain.

> The focus of a yea-sayer is—like all living things— to grow.

May God help us grow with grace, and multiply (grow others) with joy.

FOR REFLECTION AND DISCUSSION

> *For no matter how many promises God has made, they are "Yes" in Christ. And so through him the "Amen" is spoken by us to the glory of God.*
> (2 CORINTHIANS 1:20)

One. By nurture and by nature, are you more inclined to be a naysayer (a vocal skeptic) or a yea-sayer (an encouraging coach)?

Two. If you have any nay-saying tendencies, ask God's help to replace doom-and-gloom predictions with faithful and fervent prayer.

Three. If your hope has been dulled by someone else's nay-saying ways, offer those discouraging words to God and ask Him to plant within you His promises, which are "Yes" and "Amen."

Four. The focus of life is not to avoid challenges, weaknesses, or crises. The focus of all living things is to grow (and multiply). Take this thought into a time of prayer as you ask Father God to help you see as He sees.

CHOOSE TO...

STEWARD GOD'S GIFTS

My eldest son's perspective on life has often caused me to pause. On the autistic spectrum, he often sees things that others miss.

Like the time we pulled up to a stoplight and he said, "like apples."

"I'm sorry buddy, what did you say?" I asked.

"Stoplights like apples," he repeated.

And then it occurred to me: the lights are red, yellow, and green.

Or the many visits to the zoo when he spent hours absolutely mesmerized…watching the squirrels.

Or when we were on vacation in New York City and amidst the lights and sights and sounds, Jonathan was fascinated by the rain water rushing through the storm drains on every corner.

Or the countless times we have pulled out of the driveway, crested the hill, and heard a loud, "Wow! Good job, God!" as Jonathan awakened us all to a stunning sunrise or sunset.

My son has gifted us all with a fresh perspective, especially about nature. One memory in particular stands out among many in that regard.

Jonathan was ten when we were visited by a Noah-esque flood here in the Ozarks. He wanted to taste the rainwater so he reached into the cupboard and pulled out a glass mug.

I decided early on as a parent never to have anything accessible that I would mind being broken. So over the years, as uncounted glasses and dishes have broken to bits on our tile floors, the kids have heard repeatedly, "Are *you* okay? Don't worry about the dish: people are more important than things."

So that day as Jonathan was heading out the door to fill the mug with rain, though I did not care about the dish, I *was* concerned about his safety on the slippery deck.

To help him think through his choices, and in the hopes of redirecting him toward a plastic mug, I asked, "Hey buddy, what might happen if that mug fell?"

Expecting my prompt to usher in a revelation like, "Oh, I guess it could break and it might hurt me!" I waited with a smile for my brilliant teaching moment to be recognized by my son.

Instead, I was the one about to have a teaching moment.

Jonathan paused to think.

Then, with his voice filled with concern, he said, "Oh! I should get a plastic mug because if the glass mug fell, it would hurt the earth and the earth is already hurting so, so very much!"

The earth is hurting?

It was my turn to pause and think.

> *From the dawn of history, God's earth has graciously absorbed the tears of the broken.*

> *In every corner where humanity is housed, God's earth has silently witnessed all the pain we have inflicted upon one another.*

> *For millennia, God's earth has respectfully received the blood of martyrs.*

Then I remembered the Apostle Paul's wise words in his letter to the Romans:

> We know that the whole creation has been groaning as in the pains of childbirth right up to the present time. Not only so, but we ourselves, who have the firstfruits of the Spirit, groan inwardly as we wait eagerly for our adoption as sons, the redemption of our bodies. (Romans 8:22–23)

Groaning as in the pains of childbirth?

I guess that the earth *is* hurting.

(Jonathan already knew.)

FOR REFLECTION AND DISCUSSION

*The creation waits in eager expectation for the sons of God to be
revealed. For the creation was subjected to frustration, not by its
own choice, but by the will of the one who subjected it, in hope
that the creation itself will be liberated from its bondage to decay
and brought into the glorious freedom of the children of God.*
(Romans 8:19–21)

One. Personally, I have been very challenged by Jonathan's passionate
concern for God's creation. It has helped me see myself as a steward,
instead of a consumer, of the resources entrusted to me. Which affirms
the basic sensibility that when you love someone, you respect (always)
and take care of (as needed) their stuff. List the resources (the "stuff")
that God (the One you love) has entrusted to you.

Two. How well do you feel you are doing at stewarding these resources?
Write down any thoughts or ideas regarding how you can take care of
God's gifts more respectfully.

Three. The greatest physical resource God has given us is life itself. How
well are you taking care of yourself? In prayer, thank God for your life.
Ask Him to reveal any way in which you can be a better steward of the
body and time He has given you.

ADDRESS HYPOCRISY

Though I moved every year as a child, our children have only known one home. Such a difference was not planned. I did not purpose to keep my tribe rooted in one place. In fact I have happy memories of traveling as a child and exploring new cities. One home is simply how life played out as my husband and I kept following Jesus.

We live in a rural part of the Ozarks of Missouri. Our house and small acreage are surrounded by a dairy farm to the East and North and a horse ranch to the West. In other words, it can feel like we are on an Old West homestead, especially at night when the stars shine brightly.

I wish I had kept a record of all the wildlife we have seen over the years. Barry identified dozens of birds. Jonathan captured on camera a family of foxes. All of us have encountered snakes of all kinds and sizes, including a little, harmless one that greeted me one morning in the bathroom.

We have met boatloads of bugs, watched helplessly as lost cows munched our petunias, woken up to the braying of donkeys, and gazed in awe at eagles soaring and geese gliding overhead in formation.

We have seen coyotes, a wild pig, and peacocks. Turkeys and deer roam our land freely. Squirrels, mice, possum, groundhogs, and armadillos are aplenty.

But a creature I have only seen once provided a sermon illustration on integrity many years ago. I thought it was a ferret, but the sleek, seemingly cuddly critter wound up being a weasel. And (as you may have noticed) weasels are not in much demand in pet stores. As one website stated, "ferrets have been domesticated for 2,500 years, but weasels are wild pests."[10]

Weasels are brown or red-brown, furry, slender mammals that feed on mice, moles, and small birds.

They possess an interesting ability: weasels can suck the contents out of an egg without breaking its shell.

Empty, the gutted egg appears full.

Unbroken, the vacant egg seems whole.

Well fed, the weasel slips away with its deed unnoticed—for the moment.

Though instinctive and beneficial for the weasel, this ability paints a painfully accurate picture of something that is volitional and deadly for us as humans—religious hypocrisy.

The Oxford English Dictionary defines hypocrisy as "The assuming of a false appearance of virtue or goodness, with dissimulation of real character or inclinations, esp. in respect of religious life or beliefs; hence in general sense, dissimulation, pretense, sham."[11]

Some of the harshest words in the entire New Testament were directed toward hypocrisy.

Jesus vividly described spiritual shams in Matthew 23:1–33:

> They proclaim truth but do not live what they preach (v. 3).

> They tithe but neglect to exercise justice, mercy, and faith (v. 23).

> They wash the outside of their cups but fill the inside with greed and self-indulgence (v. 25).

> They are like sparkling tombs with beautiful exteriors, yet full of death within (v. 27).

When we live hypocritically, when there is a known gap between what we present outwardly and who we actually are inwardly, we leave a trail like that of the weasel's eggs.

> Though gutted, we appear full.

> Though vacant, we seem whole—for the moment.

All of us stumble and sin in many ways. God graciously extends the repentant forgiveness.

But if we teach truth and knowingly live a lie, we are in grave danger.

Weasels may trick the eyes of other mammals.

But who can escape the gaze of the all-knowing God?

FOR REFLECTION AND DISCUSSION

Cleanse me with hyssop, and I will be clean;
wash me, and I will be whiter than snow.
(PSALM 51:7)

One. Open your time of reflection by echoing David's prayer from Psalm 139:23–24: "Search me, O God, and know my heart; test me and know my anxious thoughts. See if there is any offensive way in me, and lead me in the way everlasting."

Two. Wait quietly in God's presence for a few minutes. As He searches your heart, write down any areas of concern that He brings to your attention.

Three. Take these areas into a time of repentance. You may find it helpful to change your position to focus, perhaps by kneeling or bowing your head.

Four. During this prayerful time, be mindful of any area God revealed to you that you did not want to write down.

Five. Conclude this time of cleansing with gratitude for your Forgiver, Jesus. Thank Him for His blood that washes away all sin.

CHOOSE TO...

END WELL

The mule's name was Sam. And no, this is not the beginning of a weak joke.

My husband and I spent the first seven years of our marriage as university ministers and we would often open our house during the holidays to students who could not go home.

One winter, we took two of our international students up to Barry's home in North Dakota. Historically wise, Barry had a sudden and not-so-wise idea of taking our students—one of whom was from a warm climate in the Far East—on a sleigh ride through the beautiful snowy plains of North Dakota.

So we all hopped onto a neighbor's homemade sleigh that was pulled by an unusually large mule named Sam.

After a few frozen miles, we stopped at a friend's house to warm up with a cup of hot chocolate. (Anyone who offers you hot chocolate in December in North Dakota is a friend.)

While Barry and the students were still saying good-bye, I stepped back onto the sleigh and Mr. Mule turned around and looked at me. Somewhat surprised and always analytical, I paused for a moment processing whether or not Mr. Mule might be trying to communicate with me when Sam TOOK OFF!

I lost my footing, flew up in the air, and landed flat on the sleigh. Undeterred, Mr. Mule bolted out of the driveway as I slid backwards and fell completely off the sleigh.

My back landed in a pile of fresh snow.

My head (and, obviously, my waist-length hair) also landed in something fresh—a fragrant pile of mule-poo.

Did I mention that Sam was a BIG mule??

My memory seems to have lost all surrounding details at this point.

> I do not remember the excitement we must have felt at the beginning of the sleigh ride.

> I can not describe even one piece of the stunning scenery we must have seen.

> I do not remember the family time after the ride that we no doubt had.

All of which is not surprising: we tend to remember how things end, and that ride ended in a pile of overgrown donkey dung.

Well, in some ways, life is a lot like a sleigh ride.

Whether in relationships, business endeavors, or the pursuit of dreams, what tends to stand out in our memories is *not* how excited we were in the beginning nor how dazzling we were in our prime but how those efforts ended.

So, if this moment were the moment called "end" for a project or pursuit, or even for life itself, would you and I have ended well? Or would Jesus find us—in our thoughts or in secret places—lying in a fresh, smelly mess?

God is looking for good endings. And if you are still reading this, there is still time to end well!

FOR REFLECTION AND DISCUSSION

"To him who overcomes and does my will to the end, I will give authority over the nations."
(REVELATION 2:26)

One. If today were the day called "end" for you, are there any areas you would want to clean up before presenting them to Jesus?

Two. All of us sin in many ways. But it is critically important that we not allow that reality to cause us to take sin less seriously. If you are currently aware of anything for which you need to ask God's forgiveness, pause now and take the time to come to God in repentance.

Three. Identify any "Sam-piles" that you frequently seem to stumble into: situations, places, or areas in which you are especially vulnerable to stumbling backwards. This week ask a trusted friend or mentor to partner with you in prayer for support and accountability.

BRING YOUR UNEDITED SELF TO GOD

When Jonathan was a baby, we spent time deliberating over the *What do we do about Santa Claus?* question. In the end, Jonathan's personality made the choice obvious. He was (and still is) a truth-seeking soul for whom inference is mostly a mystery. In other words, he has always needed our teachings to be clear, accurate, honest, and consistent.

So when little Keona asked about Santa Claus, the stage had already been set: "Yes, Santa Clause is real! He was a real person who lived long ago. His name was Nicholas and he did so much good that he is remembered as Saint Nicholas. He is now in heaven but his real life continues to inspire people in every generation to celebrate the spirit of generosity and give sacrificially to help others!"

Beautiful.

(Pass a tissue, please.)

Then we explained the need to just listen when other kids talked about Santa Claus because each family processed that part of Christmas in their own way. Keona smiled, nodded, and skipped away gingerly.

A few days later, though, Keona's pre-school teacher informed us that our dear daughter had reduced our beautiful explanation to just the facts.

While Ms. Laura was sharing about the wonders of Santa Claus and his soon-coming trip to visit us all, Keona sat patiently with her hand raised.

"Yes, Keona?" Ms. Laura inquired. "You've been waiting so nicely. What would you like to say?"

"Santa's dead," Keona replied.

(Silence)

Thankfully, Ms. Laura recovered quickly, saved the day, and the class survived the brutal truth.

I would have lost sleep over it all had I not still been recovering from that week's list of my eldest's questions:

> "Are you going through puberty?" (Asked of every single person at a homeschool science class.)

> "Do you have any teeth?" (Asked of the elderly gentleman being wheeled into the doctor's office.)

> "Do you have a BABY in your tummy?" (Asked of anyone, male or female, with more than a twenty-four-inch waist.)

Ah, child-speak is wonderfully unpredictable. Uncensored by long-term thinking, unedited by mistrust, the words of children lack filters and fluff.

And Jesus said,

> "I tell you the truth, unless you change and become like little children, you will never enter the kingdom of heaven. Therefore, whoever humbles himself like this child is the greatest in the kingdom of heaven." (Matthew 18:3–4)

No, I do not believe Jesus was giving us license to offend all our neighbors.

I believe Jesus was challenging us to come to Him without pretense.

Bringing our unedited selves to God can be humbling. We often prefer to clean up first. But in reality, such delays serve only to hinder true transformation.

When we come to God vulnerably, without censoring our feelings, with our words honest and clumsy, we acknowledge and lean on three glorious truths:

God knows us intimately,
    God forgives us fully, and
        God loves us completely.

FOR REFLECTION AND DISCUSSION

Here is a trustworthy saying that deserves full acceptance: Christ
Jesus came into the world to save sinners—of whom I am the worst.
But for that very reason I was shown mercy so that in me, the worst
of sinners, Christ Jesus might display his unlimited patience as an
example for those who would believe in him and receive eternal life.
(1 TIMOTHY 1:15–16)

One. All of us remember times when we would have gladly retracted our words had we been given the opportunity. A child's lack of pretense may be somewhat startling, but as adults, a lack of discretion can be disastrous. How wonderful that we can bring our unedited selves to God! Open your time of prayer with gratitude that you can be yourself in His presence.

Two. Consider Paul's advice to Timothy in the passage above. Paul, the world's most famous missionary, felt that he needed, and therefore displayed, God's "unlimited patience." Paul came to God without pretense: he knew he was a sinner. Why might someone want to avoid being vulnerable before God?

Three. Paul continued by exclaiming: "Now to the King eternal, immortal, invisible, the only God, be honor and glory for ever and ever. Amen." (1 Timothy 1:17) Taking into consideration verses 15-16, what do you think motivated such a shout of praise to God in verse 17?

CHOOSE TO...

SHARE THE JOURNEY

What on earth is going on with the weather? I wondered when the view suddenly clouded with dust. As the winds kicked up, my hands tightened on the wheel and I began to silently pray.

Leah, in the passenger seat, watched with mounting concern as bits of debris began to blow across the road. Sarah, in the backseat wrestling with a map, was oblivious to the changing weather conditions around us.

My relationship with these two amazing women began with mentoring and grew into lifelong friendship. Mentally fierce, emotionally honest, adventurous, and hilarious, they kept me laughing and sometimes traveled with me to my speaking engagements when my kids were small.

Such was the case on this day as we made our way to Texas for a retreat. We left home in plenty of time to arrive and speak at the opening session. But what we did not account for in our timing was driving straight into the path of a tornado convergence just South of downtown Dallas.

Imagine, if you can, a day before the advent of real-time weather apps. The storm came up so suddenly—we had no idea what was happening.

"I think we missed our turn back there," Sarah offered calmly from the backseat. Then Leah—who had just spied a funnel cloud—gripped my arm and screamed, "I-think-I-see-a-TOR-NAAAA-DOOOOOO!!!"

"Why is everyone screaming?" Sarah asked. And then she looked up.

Though we now can laugh retelling the story, in the moment we were all terrified. And the next thing that happened might have been equally terrifying for Leah and Sarah. They heard something they had never heard before or since: me shouting!

"IS THERE ANYONE IN THE NEXT LANE?!" I yelled.

Though Leah is, indisputably, the queen, Sarah and I both have a good dose of drama running through our veins. In the ensuing minutes, all three of us prayer-shouted our way off the highway, onto the access road, and into the safety of a nearby building where we waited out the storm.

An hour later we returned to the car and drove very slowly to the campground, entirely missing my first session but eventually arriving at our destination filled with gratitude for safety and especially for one another.

One another.

It is what makes storms of any kind bearable.

Tornados can come in many different shapes.

The physical ones tear up land and houses.

The emotional ones tear up hearts and homes.

Leah, Sarah, and I drove through a physical one that day in Texas. But I am sure many of us are driving through emotional ones right now.

It is startling when life is so obviously out of our control.

It is unnerving when no amount of planning can silence a storm.

But it is infinitely better to weather such storms with others, especially with somewhat dramatic prayer-shouting friends.

Find a friend.

And together, pray your way to safety.

FOR REFLECTION AND DISCUSSION

I thank my God every time I remember you.
(PHILIPPIANS 1:3)

One. Jesus does not offer faith for independent study. Christianity is lived in the plural not the singular. Some choose to drive solo spiritually in an attempt to protect themselves from interpersonal pain. But simply put: we are safer together than alone.

Two. If you currently find yourself within a storm, prayerfully consider the following: Are your current choices protecting you or making you more vulnerable? Is anything distracting you from choosing the safest path for your soul? Does anyone else know what you are facing?

Three. Take a few moments to bring to mind the names and faces of a few prayer-shouting friends in your life. Pray for each one with gratitude for their lives and love.

CHOOSE TO…

ATTEND TO ROOTS

"Why did the snow leopard turn out to be evil, Mom?" five-year-old Keona asked with a worried tone.

Turning off the oatmeal on the stove, I picked up a pad of paper and a pen to settle into a mentoring moment with my beloved daughter. Most teaching moments are unexpected, but I saw this one coming within the first few minutes of watching a new movie one family-night.

An infant was placed on the doorstep of a good man, a kung fu master, who "raised the child as his own." But the baby boy grew to be a powerful, evil warrior.

Amidst the humor and excellent animation, a disturbing question arose for my children: How can someone with "good" parents grow to become a "bad" person?

> For adults, the answer is sobering: choice is a destiny-shaper.

> For children, such an answer can be paralyzing.

So I responded with pictures.

Drawing a tree from the trunk up, I said, "Keona, Mommy is drawing a tree filled with fruit. What kind of fruit tree do you want it to be?"

"An orange tree!" she said with wide eyes, "But, Mommy, you forgot the roots."

"That's on purpose, babe. Here, first help me fill the tree with fruit."

When our tree was loaded with oranges, I drew two small roots at the bottom and asked, "What would happen if a tree with all this fruit only had two short, little roots?"

"It would fall down," she said quickly.

"You're right. In fact, roots underground are two to three times broader than the tree branches," I offered while drawing the roots that would be needed to support such a fruit-laden tree.

Labeling the tree, I said, "Well, in my illustration: fruit equal giftings and roots equal virtue. The snow leopard had many gifts. He was fast, smart, and skilled at kung fu. But he spent more time developing his giftings than developing virtues like love, joy, peace, patience, kindness, goodness, faithfulness, gentleness, and self-control. So what happened to his life?"

"It fell down," Keona replied, staring at the drawing.

Then she looked into my eyes and her brow relaxed. I could see it in her eyes—our outrageously gifted daughter understood why we place such emphasis on virtue in our family.

"Can I have maple syrup in my oatmeal?" she inquired, without missing a beat. "Yes, my love," I replied, turning on the stove once again.

But lest I wonder if the lesson was heard, dear Keona said softly to herself, "I'll keep this tree picture in my journal."

P.S. It was some of the best oatmeal we have ever shared.

FOR REFLECTION AND DISCUSSION

*"A farmer went out to sow his seed.... Some fell on rocky places,
where it did not have much soil. It sprang up quickly, because
the soil was shallow. But when the sun came up, the plants
were scorched, and they withered because they had no root."*
(Matthew 13:3, 5–6)

One. Nature, nurture, and free will are at the heart of an age-old debate. Review your own childhood and identify (1) one strength that you inherited from your family, (2) one weakness that you did not inherit from your family, and (3) one personal choice that is utterly unique in your family.

Two. Reflect on the orange tree illustration. Whether or not you feel laden with fruit, what adjectives would you use to describe your root system? For example, deep, shallow, narrow, broad, fragile, established, vulnerable, sturdy?

Three. Reflect on the fate of the second seed in Jesus' parable from Matthew 13:3, 5–6. Contrast the difference between what people saw above ground and what was really happening below ground.

Four. In soil and souls, roots grow where seeds are planted. And seeds are planted through the power of choice. As you come to the end of *Every Choice is a Seed*, look back over the choices that stood out to you. Offer these choices to God in love, thanking Him for valuing the hidden growth of virtue above the public display of giftings in your life.

May God help us to plant our choice-seeds well.

In Him,

Alicia

NOTES

1. Brother Lawrence, *The Practice of the Presence of God* (Springdale, PA: Whitaker House, 1982), 81.

2. Brother Lawrence, *The Practice of the Presence of God* (Springdale, PA: Whitaker House, 1982), 80–81.

3. Bridgid Herman. *Creative Prayer* (New York, NY: Cosimo Classics, 2007), 5.

4. Henri J. M. Nouwen, *Making All Things New: An Invitation to the Spiritual Life* (San Francisco, CA: HarperCollins Publishers, 1981), 71.

5. "holy, adj. and n." *OED Online*, Oxford University Press, December 2020, www.oed.com/view/Entry/87833. Accessed 6 January 2021.

6. "Worship." *Merriam-Webster.com Dictionary*, Merriam-Webster, https://www.merriam-webster.com/dictionary/worship. Accessed 6 Jan. 2021.

7. This illustration is from Richard Swenson. *Margin: Restoring Emotional, Physical, Financial, and Time Reserves to Overloaded Lives* (Colorado Springs, CO: NavPress, 2004)

8. This content was excerpted from Alicia Britt Chole, *Until The Whole World Knows* (Rogersville, MO: onewholeworld, 2000).

9. Dr. George O. Wood, circa 2001.

10. https://sciencing.com/differences-between-ferrets-weasels-8753674.html Accessed January 9, 2021.

11. "hypocrisy, n." *OED Online*, Oxford University Press, December 2020, www.oed.com/view/Entry/90491. Accessed 9 January 2021.

If you enjoyed *Every Choice is a Seed*,
you'll love reading Alicia's other books!

To explore her writings, learn more about the
Chole's ministry, or follow Alicia on social media, visit

www.aliciachole.com

aliciabrittchole

aliciabrittcholeauthor

aliciachole